COMPLETE CATALOGUE OF

FORD CARS

IN BRITAIN

COMPLETE CATALOGUE OF
FORD CARS

IN BRITAIN
from Model T to Fiesta

David Burgess-Wise

BAY VIEW BOOKS

Published 1991 by
Bay View Books Ltd
13a Bridgeland Street
Bideford, Devon EX39 2QE

© Copyright 1991 by Bay View Books Ltd

Designed by Peter Laws

ISBN 1 870979 25 7
Printed in Hong Kong

Contents

V8-40 at Monte Carlo, 1935

Dagenham's millionth car was this 1946 Prefect ▼

Foreword

Few motor companies can have fulfilled their founder's dreams as fully as Ford. Henry Ford, born the son of an Irish immigrant farmer in Michigan in 1863 – coincidentally the same year as another famous motoring Henry, whose surname was Royce – had the vision of building a "car for the great multitude". In the nine decades since he founded his company, it has made cars by the hundreds of millions; in Britain, where Ford production began in a converted tram factory in Manchester in 1911, over 20 million Fords have been built, double the number made by any other marque.

There used to be an advertising slogan that claimed "there's a Ford in your future", and for many British motorists there has been a Ford in their past. A generation learnt to drive on the old sidevalve Fords; their children have fond memories of the family Cortina or Anglia.

This is the story of British Fords up to 1980; and while it is principally concerned with the cars built after the Second World War, it also deals with the earlier British Fords, for as late as 1959 Ford in Britain was still building cars that were recognisably descended from the first Ford manufactured in their country, the Model T.

The Ford stand at the 1953 Motor Show

◄ Interior of the 1953 Anglia offered "extreme comfort"

Zephyr in the 1953 RAC Rally ▼

The new 1962 Cortina arrives at a dealership

Launching "the World's Most Exciting Light Car", 1959 ▼

◄ Export model Mk II Cortina two door goes for export

New lamps and ▲ bumpers for 1980 Cortina

In writing it, I have referred as much as possible to contemporary sources, and the production statistics have been compiled from the factory records. One problem has been that in the old days, minute records were kept by the production staff; but Ford was one of the first companies to use computers for record work and computer records were – sadly – often transient. So while it was easy to count the numbers of individual derivatives built before the 1970s, after that point the permanent records often only refer to broader categories.

It can also be difficult to determine overall production of particular cars because at one period many cars were built as kits of parts for overseas assembly ("KD" – for "knocked down") while others were exported "built up" ("BU"). Where these figures are available, I have added them in to the total. One thing you can be sure of: production totals from one source rarely agree exactly with those from another!

Like many of my generation, I first met Ford cars through the trusty small sidevalves that were so common in the years just after the war; then my uncle bought a new Consul in 1951 and I still remember the thrill of seeing the speedometer needle touch 60mph as we drove north from Brighton! My connection with Fords has filled the major part of my working life and I've been lucky enough to know many of the men who have guided the fortunes of the British Ford company during the period covered by this book.

No other make engenders such enthusiasm as Ford; of the 350 antique car clubs in Britain, 40 are for Ford owners. This book is dedicated to them.

David Burgess-Wise, April 1991

Both ends of the
British-built Model T
spectrum. A 1912
Manchester-bodied
two-seater . . .

. . . and a 1927 Coupé.
Stylistically very
different, but
almost identical
mechanically

Model A Fordor,
1930

Full load for a 1928
Model A Roadster

Model T 1908-27

Henry's "Universal Car" had its world show premiere at Olympia in 1908 so it's hardly surprising that the first assembly plant outside North America was established in Britain in October 1911 and produced its 250,000th car in April 1925.

SPECIFICATION

Engine in-line 2890cc sv four cylinder
Bore × stroke 95×101.5mm
Maximum power 20bhp @ 1800rpm
Transmission two speed epicyclic
Chassis pressed steel channel
Wheelbase 100.5in (2553mm)
Track 57in (1447mm)
Length 134in (3404mm)
Suspension transverse leaf front/ rear
Brakes two wheel mechanical
Bodywork Roadster, Tourer, Tudor, Fordor, Town Car
Maximum speed (approx) 42mph (68km/h)
Total production (Britain) 300,000

Model A and its derivatives

Model A 1928-32 When Henry Ford was eventually convinced that the Model T had had its day, production was halted at the end of May 1927 in Detroit and development started on a successor. However, Model Ts continued to be built until August in Manchester and to the end of December in Cork, Ireland. The new Model A was first shown publicly at the end of 1927, and in its styling and specification was as modern as the Model T had been archaic (though it still retained transverse springing). But Henry Ford's vision of a "Universal Car" the same the world over had run its course with Model T, and the new Model A, with an engine of more than 3 litres, was totally out of kilter with the mood in Europe, where cars were taxed on the size of their engines. The introduction of a smaller, 2033cc engine in what was known as Model AF was intended to solve this problem (at an extra cost of £5!). However, the AF engine was still bigger and thirstier than those of its rivals, though it offered nothing extra in the way of performance; it was quite the wrong car for Europe during the Depression. As an indication of this, the vast new factory at Dagenham, opened on October 1, 1931, built just five Model A cars during its first three months of operation. Trucks took up some of the slack, fortunately, and one of them, AA4791110, was the first vehicle built at Dagenham . . .

SPECIFICATION

Engine 2033cc (AF)/3285cc (A) in-line sv four cylinder
Bore × stroke 77.5×108mm (AF); 98×108mm (A)
Maximum power 40bhp @ 2200rpm
Transmission three speed
Chassis pressed steel channel
Wheelbase 103.5in (2629mm)
Track 56in (1422mm)
Length 132in (3353mm)
Suspension transverse leaf front/ rear
Brakes four wheel mechanical
Bodywork Roadster, Cabriolet, Tourer, Tudor, Fordor
Maximum speed (approx) AF 54mph (87km/h)/A 65mph (105km/h)
Total production (Britain) 14,516

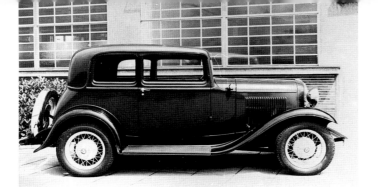

V8-18 Tudor

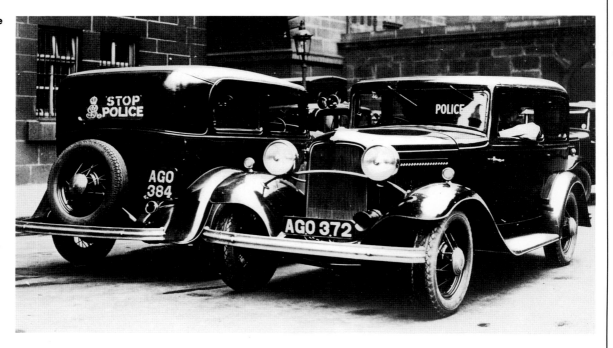

1933 Model BF Police
Car

Model B 1932-34 Ford insisted that their new model was called "improved Model A" and codenamed it "AB" but everyone else called it the Model B – which unfortunately meant that the smallbore version was called "BF" . . . The engine was redesigned in the interests of efficiency and the fuel tank was moved from the scuttle to the rear of the car; Magna big-hub wheels with balloon tyres and improved body styling – Briggs were the "on-site" body builders – were other obvious differences and *The Autocar* thought that "the new models are as far ahead of the Model A in general elegance as was 'A' in front of 'T'". But times were hard and "general elegance" wasn't as important as operating economy – on which Model B was sadly deficient. Had Model B and its sister, the new V8, been Ford's only 1932 offering, the recently-opened Dagenham works would have gone broke . . .

SPECIFICATION

Engine 2033cc (ABF)/3285cc (AB) in-line sv four cylinder
Bore × stroke 77.5×108mm (ABF); 98×108mm (AB)
Maximum power 41bhp @ 3000rpm (ABF); 48bhp @ 2400rpm (AB)
Transmission three speed

Chassis pressed steel channel
Wheelbase 106in (2692mm)
Track 56in (1422mm)
Length 142in (3607mm)
Suspension transverse leaf front/rear
Brakes four wheel mechanical
Bodywork Roadster, Cabriolet, Tourer, Tudor, Fordor
Maximum speed (approx) AF 57mph (87km/h)/A 65mph (105km/h)
Total production (Britain) 8784

1932 Model B Tudor

30hp V8 and its derivatives

V8-18 1932-33 The first Ford V8s sold in Britain were actually Canadian-built; it wasn't until 1935 that the Dagenham foundry began making V8 power units. In any case, demand for such a relatively large-engined car – its taxable horse-power was 30 – was not sufficiently high in those Depression years to justify full production at Dagenham. The earliest were the best – middle-aged spread affected the line from 1936 on – but the whippy 1932 chassis was not really adequate for the performance which, *The Autocar* enthused , "up to nearly 80mph . . . can be equalled by very few machines on the road today, even by those of sports type".

Available October 1932 – October 1933

SPECIFICATION

Engine 3622cc sv V8
Bore × stroke 77.8×95mm
Transmission three speed
Maximum power 65bhp @ 3800rpm
Chassis pressed steel channel
Suspension transverse leaf front/rear
Wheelbase 106in (2692mm)

1934 V8-40 with British (Jensen?) sports bodywork

V8-40 Cabriolet

Track 56in (1422mm)
Length 142in (3607mm)
Brakes four wheel mechanical
Bodywork Cabriolet, Tudor, Fordor
Maximum speed (approx) 78mph (125km/h)
Total production (Britain) 911 (inc V8-40)

V8-40 1933-34 The handsomest of all the Ford V8s and the first actually to be produced in Europe, since it was assembled in Cologne and Cork, Ireland. British sales, however, were negligible. A double-drop X-braced chassis cured the handling deficiencies of Model 18. Ford-Britain only introduced the Model 40 in October 1933 – eight months after America – so all British-market Model 40s had the skirted wings that were the main external difference between 1933 and '34 models.

Available October 1933 – June 1934

Specification as above except:
Maximum power 80bhp @ 3500rpm
Wheelbase 112in (2845mm)
Length 176in (4470mm)
Maximum speed 81mph (130km/h)
Bodywork Tudor, Fordor
Total production (Britain) see Model 18

1932 V8-18 Coupé

1935 V8-48 Fordor Sedan

V8-68s as far as the eye can see

V8-48 1935 More forward-mounted engine gave the V8-48 a rather nose-heavy appearance. The first Ford V8 to be built at Dagenham, it did not go into production here until seven months after it had been launched in Dearborn! The first Dagenham-built V8 engine, completed on July 17, 1935, was numbered 1792301; the first car left the line on July 25. A welcome addition to the line-up was the "Utility Car" with handsome varnished wood shooting brake bodywork.

Available March 12 – November 21, 1935

Specification as above except:
Length 183in (4650mm)
Maximum speed 86mph (138km/h)
Bodywork Tudor, Fordor, Utility Car
Total production (Britain) 616

V8-68 1935-36 At last Dagenham was catching up on V8 launch timing: the more rounded Model 68 appeared only a month after its American counterpart and was the best-selling 30hp Ford V8 model of the 1930s.

Produced November 12, 1935 – December 30, 1936

Specification as above except:
Track 55in (1397mm)
Length 185in (4700mm)
Maximum speed 84mph (135km/h)
Total production (Britain) 4527

V8-78 1937-38 With more than a hint of Lincoln-Zephyr about its styling, the daringly streamlined Model 78 challenged Model 40 as the best-looking V8 line. Cable brakes were new – though not necessarily an improvement!

Produced January 25, 1937 – June 10, 1938
Specification as above except:
Maximum speed 87mph (140km/h)
Bodywork: Club Cabriolet added
Total production (Britain) 4331

V8-81A 1938 Dagenham was once again out of kilter with Dearborn on introduction times, but perhaps it was just as well, for the lines of the V8-81A lacked the "showroom appeal" of its predecessor.

Produced April 22 – November 22, 1938
Specification as above
Total production (Britain) 1200

V8-91A 1938-40 With similar styling to the new Mercury line introduced by Ford-US, the V8-91A broke new ground for Ford by featuring hydraulic brakes – though old Henry Ford had always vaunted "the safety of steel from toe to wheel" as a plus point.

Produced December 13, 1938 – January 16, 1940
Total production (Britain) 1878

1937 V8-78 Fordor sedan

1936 V8-68 Tudor

1939 V8-91A Convertible Cabriolet

The 1938 V8-81A was only built in De Luxe form in Britain

1948 Pilot saloon

V8 Pilot E71A 1947-51 Dagenham's first "new" model after the war was a real scissors and paste job, created after a proposed all-new 14.9hp V8 had failed to materialise. It took the bodyshell of the pre-war 22hp V8-62, made more imposing by a new high-fronted bonnet and radiator grille designed by the engineering chief of Briggs Motor Bodies, Australian-born Don Ward. It would have had a new 2.5 litre V8 engine, too – indeed, the model was launched to Ford dealers in this form in the summer of 1947 – but the new power unit proved so gutless that a hasty switch was made to the tried, tested – and thirsty – 30hp V8, of which Dagenham had already built over 250,000 for war vehicles.

In an era of austerity and vehicle and fuel rationing, the Pilot seemed like totally the wrong car for the times, but its effortless progress endeared it to those who could obtain an extra petrol allowance, like doctors and farmers. King George VI was a Pilot fan, too, and his specially commissioned shooting brake – the last car he ordered – survives in the Royal Motor Museum at Sandringham. Built on a long-wheelbase chassis, this car handles more like a state barge than normal Pilots! It also has a one-of-a-kind floor shift rather than the standard steering column gear change.

A bizarre feature of the Pilot was its

1951 Pilot Pick-up, bodied by Reynolds of Dagenham

1951 long wheelbase Garner-bodied Pilot shooting brake for King George VI ▼

The standard V8 Pilot shooting brake ▼

1950 Pilot Police Car

V8 Pilots with metal estate bodywork for Kenya Police ▼

braking system, which combined hydraulic front and mechanical rear operation but built-in hydraulic jacks were a feature seen on no other Ford. A useful improvement was the provision of a vacuum reservoir for the suction-operated windscreen wipers, which removed the old Ford bugbear of the vacuum wiper action dying away in top gear, just when it was needed most! Production of shooting brakes (built by outside specialists like Garner or Perry) and pick-ups continued into 1952 on the E71C commercial chassis.

Produced July 16, 1947 – May 29, 1951 (E71A 7189001 – E71A 7255082)

Engine 3622cc sv V8
Bore × stroke 77.8×95.3mm
Maximum power 85bhp @ 3500rpm
Transmission three speed manual
Chassis pressed steel channel
Suspension transverse leaf
Brakes four wheel Girling hydraulic/mechanical
Bodywork four door saloon
Length 175in (4445mm)
Track 56in (1422mm)
Wheelbase 108in (2743mm)
Maximum speed (approx) 83mph (133km/h)
Total production 21,487 BU, 668 KD

GRAND TOTAL PRODUCTION 30HP V8: (BRITAIN) 35,618

The 1935 V8-60 was a 22hp version of the V8-48

Aviatrix Amy Johnson drove this V8-62 in the 1939 Monte Carlo Rally

22hp V8 and its derivatives

V8-60 1935-36 An oddball model that even people who worked at Ford in the 1930s tend to have forgotten, this was nothing more than a Model 48 fitted with the 22hp "Alsace" V8 originally designed for the French "Matford" and only introduced in the US in 1937. Apart from the power unit, the only difference between Models 48 and 60 was a lower final drive ratio.

Produced September 1, 1935 – June 26, 1936

SPECIFICATION

Engine 2227cc sv V8
Bore × stroke 66×81.28mm
Maximum power 60bhp @ 3500rpm
Transmission three speed
Chassis pressed steel channel
Wheelbase 112in (2845mm)
Track 56in (1422mm)
Length 183in (4650mm)
Suspension transverse leaf front/rear
Brakes four wheel mechanical
Bodywork Fordor
Maximum speed (approx) 70mph (113km/h)
Total production (Britain) 2807

V8-62 1936-41 An even closer link with Matford, this one, for the bodywork was identical to that of the French car, though it was produced by Briggs Bodies on the Dagenham estate. It had a new chassis frame, which gave a 2.5in reduction in overall height. A slightly higher final drive ratio (4.55:1 instead of 4.77:1) than Model 60 was used. The luggage compartment on the first Model 62 bodies was only accessible from inside the car, an external hinged panel giving access to the spare wheel only; from September 1937 there was an opening boot, with the spare wheel carried in a recess on its lid.

Produced June 24, 1936 – February 3, 1941

Specification as above except:
Length 173in (4395mm)
Total production (Britain) 9239 (BU 7869, KD 1550)

The V8-62 at Ford's 1936 Albert Hall Exhibition

Extended boot of 1937 Model 62

1934 Model Y Fordor

**Prototype Model 19,
February 1932**

◄ **The Model Y-based
1932 Puttock
Special**

▲ **Model Y Tudor,
1932. Note straight
bumper and "short"**

**radiator compared
with 1934 car in top
picture**

The first production
Model Y, 1932

Model Y and its derivatives

Ford 8/10 1932-59 The longest-running "bloodline" in Ford of Britain history was that of the Ford 8/10 series, in production with a virtually unchanged specification from 1932 to 1959. Indeed, this mechanical coelacanth had several features that would not have been unfamiliar to the owner of a 1909 Model T – transverse leaf springs fore and aft, located by tie rods, a monobloc sidevalve engine with a detachable cylinder head, mechanically-operated brakes (though at least these were on all four wheels rather than the rear-wheels-only fitment of Model T). The author can recall marvelling in the 1960s at the fact that the near-new Ford Populars he was following on the road were less advanced mechanically than the 1927 Clyno tourer he was using as everyday transport at the time!

Model Y 8hp 1932-37 Remarkably, the original Model Y – or Model 19, as it was the next project Henry Ford undertook after his immortal Model 18 V8 – was created in Dearborn, from drawing board to prototype, between October 1931 and February 1932 and was in full production in the new Dagenham factory in August 1932. The reason for the urgency was the total collapse of Model A sales in the depression and the very real threat of Dagenham having to close as a result; with its attractive styling, the Model Y gave Ford over 40 per cent of the 8hp market, and was copied by both Morris and Singer. Neither company, though, could match the £100 price tag on the Model Y Populars produced from October 1935 – the first and only four-seater saloon car to be offered at so low a price.

Standard factory products were two- and four-door saloons; several outside companies – most notably Jensen – produced neat tourers on the Model Y chassis but these were not entirely approved of by the factory since it was felt that they lacked the rigidity of the saloon.

The first year's production had the "short rad" and straight bumpers; cars built from October 1933 (Y37291) had a long radiator shell and dip-centre bumpers like the contemporary V8-40. Steering was vague, particularly at the upper end of the Y's modest speed range, and prone to wander towards the crown of the road camber, but this remarkably tough little car gave many motorists their first taste of new-car motoring.

Produced August 1932 – August 31, 1937 (Y0001 – Y199333)

SPECIFICATION

Engine 933cc in-line four cylinder sv
Bore × stroke 56.6×92.5mm
Maximum power 23.4bhp @ 4000rpm
Transmission three speed
Chassis pressed steel channel
Wheelbase 90in (2286mm)
Track 45in (1143mm)
Length 143in (3632mm)
Suspension transverse leaf front/rear
Brakes four wheel mechanical
Bodywork Tudor, Fordor
Maximum speed (approx) 59mph (95km/h)
Total production (Britain) 135,244 BU, 22,424 KD

The 1937 7Y Ford "Eight"

7Y "Eight" in the showroom

The £100 Model Y Popular, 1935

It can be yours –

THE £100 FORD SALOON

Model 7Y 8hp 1937-39 Though this model was only produced for a couple of years, it (and its 7W stablemate) were remarkable in being the first British-built Fords to have their bodywork entirely designed in England – much against the instructions of Dearborn. But the design was accepted by Henry Ford and the young manager who had been deputed to take the prototypes to the USA for approval – Patrick Hennessy – would eventually become chairman of Ford of Britain and the moving spirit behind some of its most successful designs in the 1950s and 60s.

Chassis of the 7Y and 7W were new, too, with a longer spring base for better ride and handling, while "easy clean" disc wheels replaced the welded-spoke wire wheels of the earlier cars. The standard 7Y was announced in August 1937, while a De Luxe version appeared in October, with twin wipers, clock, ashtrays, a metal cover for the spare wheel, plated hub caps and screen surround, trafficators and a glovebox lid. Running boards were deleted from the standard model in October 1938.

Produced September 1, 1937 – September 20, 1939 (Y199334 – Y278542)

Specification as above except:
Length 148in (3760mm)
Bodywork Tudor
Total production (Britain) 59,598 BU, 5500 KD

Anglia 8hp E04A 1939-48 First to bear a famous name, the Anglia was unusual in being introduced after the outbreak of war in 1939. Basically a more square-cut derivative of the 7Y, only 5136 (2961 BU and 2175 KD) were built before war stopped production in 1941. The war also put paid to a project to build a de luxe coupé version of the Anglia with independent front suspension. Two prototypes were built; one survives. Production began again on May 25, 1945, less than three weeks after VE-Day, and the first complete car left Dagenham on June 21.

De Luxe Anglias had running boards and an opening windscreen, but postwar models all lacked these features. However, they gained 10in brakes in place of the prewar 8in front/7in rear drums. Another plus point was the fact that the Anglia was Britain's cheapest car at £293; the bad news was that the postwar Labour government's export-or-die policy meant that very few were seen on the home market. For export to territories where there was no tax on engine capacity, Anglias were fitted with the 1172cc 10hp power unit; for North America, a front bench seat was also specified, along with the three-aperture 7W grille. The Anglias sold on the

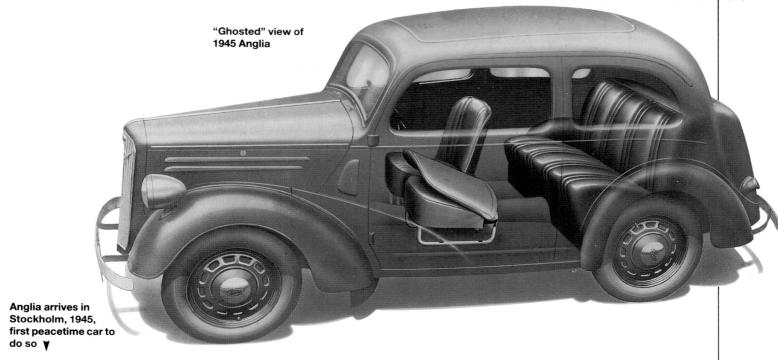

"Ghosted" view of 1945 Anglia

Anglia arrives in Stockholm, 1945, first peacetime car to do so ▼

1940 Anglia 8hp EO4A with blackout masks on the headlamps

The 1945 Anglia EO4A lacked running boards ▼

British market kept the squarer radiator shell, which was given a restyled grille surround with a broad upper strip carrying the name "Anglia" from December 1947. Direction indicators were standardised from April 1948.

Produced October 31, 1939 – November 3, 1948 (Y278543 – Y369249)
Last wartime Anglia Y287241
First postwar Anglia Y291482

Specification as above except:
Length 152in (3860mm)
Maximum speed 60mph (97km/h)
Total production (Britain) 46,745 BU, 9062 KD

1950 Martin Walter "Utilecon" estate car built on the E494C commercial chassis

1949 Anglia 8hp E494A undergoing service

Film star Jean Kent and her Anglia E494A ▼

1950 Anglia rallied by the Reece cousins from Liverpool ◄

Anglia 8hp E494A 1948-53 Possibly the only time that the motor industry has reintroduced the model-before-last as a new design, the 1949 Anglia was almost identical in appearance to the 1937 7Y, apart from a small protruding luggage boot and a grille which differed only in having twin apertures – rather like the BMW grille – instead of the single opening of the 7Y. Even though its low price – making the Anglia by far the cheapest "real" car on the British market – caused much to be forgiven, there was now real criticism of its an-

tediluvian handling; *Autocar* was as scathing as the conventions of the day allowed: "Over some surfaces there is a comparatively sharp, short pitching action, and when the car is taken around bends at all fast, a rather curious corner movement is evident, while an up and down motion is set up on surfaces which with other types of suspension are regarded nowadays as smooth." Now the only external difference between the domestic and export Anglias was the radiator badge, export models being badged "1.17 litre".

Produced October 27, 1948 – October 13, 1953 (Y369250 – Y470841)

Specification as above
Total production (Britain) 83,027 BU, 25,751 KD

GRAND TOTAL PRODUCTION 8HP: 387,351

Model C and Model Y
on the line at
Dagenham, 1934

Special black/ivory
paint job for the De
Luxe Model C 10hp

Model C 10hp 1934-35 Another Dearborn design, the Model C (or Model 20 in Dearborn parlance) was to the V8-48 as Model Y was to V8-40 – a miniature stylistic clone. Its rounded lines brought it the nickname "Barrel Ford", though Dagenham referred to it as the "De Luxe Ford". Its robust sidevalve engine was dimensionally similar to and had the same stroke as that of the Model Y so the same production machinery could be used. Early examples of Model C had a pressed steel "punt" chassis: speed king Malcolm Campbell (recently appointed a director of Ford Motor Company), praised the lively performance of the C, which was the fastest of all the 10hp line. Dearborn spoke of bringing out a version powered by a small V8 engine, but it failed to materialise. The announcement dates of the various models were as follows: Fordor September and Tudor October 1934; Tourer May 1935.

Produced October 1, 1934 – October 31, 1935 (C001 – C23931)

Engine in-line 1172cc four cylinder sv
Bore × stroke 63.5×92.56mm
Maximum power 30bhp @ 4000rpm
Transmission three speed
Chassis pressed steel channel
Wheelbase 90in (2286mm)
Track 45in (1143mm)
Length 147in (3734mm)
Suspension transverse leaf front/rear
Brakes four wheel mechanical
Bodywork Tourer, Tudor, Fordor
Maximum speed (approx) 70mph (113km/h)
Total production (Britain) 17,641 BU, 3699 KD (7587 Tudor, 9657 Fordor, 1068 Tourer)

Main distinguishing
feature of the 1935
Model CX was the
bars across the grille

Rarest version of the
Model CX was this
tourer

Model CX 1935-37 A minor facelift
for the Model C and chiefly recognisa-
ble by triple horizontal bars across the
radiator grille and redesigned bonnet
louvres similar to those of the contemporary V8-48.

Produced October 15, 1935 – March 22,
1937 (C23932 – C70533)
Fordor introduced October, Tudor introduced November, Tourer introduced
January 1936

Specification as above
Total production (Britain) 29,919
BU, 7734 KD (14,929 Tudor, 13,011
Fordor, 1795 Tourer)

Spare wheel cover
was a feature of the
Ford "Ten" Model 7W
10hp, seen with 1939
V8-81 cabriolet

Model 7W 10hp 1937-38 With the
7Y, the first example of "home-grown"
styling from Dagenham. Distinguished
from the 7Y by its "three-hole" radiator
grille. An improvement was an extra 4in
in the wheelbase and a greater spring
base (achieved by mounting the front
spring almost 3in ahead of its axle and
the flatter rear spring 6in behind the
back axle) which improved the ride.
Performance was similar to the superse-
ded model.

Produced March 22 1937 – September 29,
1938 (C70534 – C150197)
Fordor announced February, Tudor announced April, Tourer announced May

Specification as above except:
Length 156in (3962mm)
Wheelbase 94in (2388mm)
Bodywork Tudor, Fordor, Tourer
Total production (Britain) 31,717
BU, 9948 KD (10,703 Tudor, 18,983
Fordor, 1639 Tourer)

1937 Model 7W Ford
"Ten" Tudor

1939 version of the "Ten Ahead of its Class" – the E93A Prefect

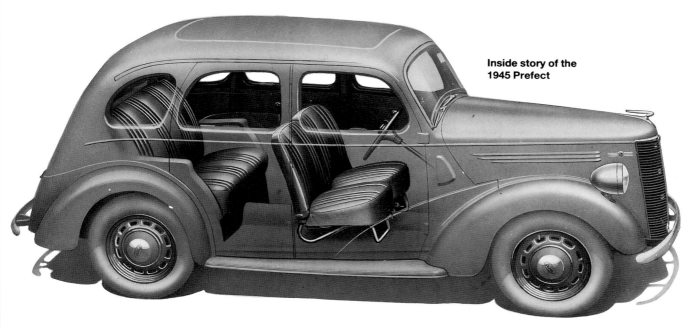

Inside story of the 1945 Prefect

E93A Prefect was the millionth car built at Dagenham

Prefect 10hp E93A 1938-49 Billed as "the Ten at the head of its class", the Prefect was the first Ford model anywhere to have a name instead of a series letter. Though it was mechanically almost identical to the 7W, the Prefect had "far more imposing lines", thanks mainly to a new streamlined radiator grille whose "blunt prow" was set well ahead of the radiator proper. A "crocodile bonnet" was another significant change; inside, the car was only altered in respect of the colour of the plastic mouldings used for the window surrounds and fascia panel. Stronger bumpers permitted the use of a pillar-type bumper jack.

Produced October 3, 1938 – January 26, 1949 (C150197 – C403099)
All models introduced October except Coupé (February 1939)

Specification as above except:
Length 155.5in (3950mm)
Maximum speed 65mph (105km/h)
Bodywork Tourer, Tudor, Fordor, Coupé
Total production (Britain) 120,505 BU (includes 1028 tourers, 667 coupés, 10,163 Tudors), 37,502 KD

Rarest version of the 1939 Prefect was the Drop Head Coupé

Launched in 1948,
the E493A Prefect
had inset headlamps

Prefect 10hp E493A 1948-53 Announced at the October 1948 Earls Court Show, the E493A Prefect differed only in appearance from the previous model. Chief external change was the adoption of more voluminous front wings incorporating the combined head/side lamp units and a taller chromed radiator grille reminiscent of that fitted to the V8 Pilot. Swivelling instead of fixed scuttle vents and the elimination of the swage line across the lower part of the front door were other differentiating features.

Produced December 21, 1948 – September 30, 1953 (C403100 – C740843)

Specification as above except:
Bodywork Fordor
Maximum speed 68mph (110km/h)
Total production (Britain) 117,206 BU, 75,023 KD

Overloaded Prefect
on the Monte Carlo
Rally

Press launch of the
103E Popular,
October 1953

The 103E was a more basic version of the Export Anglia, with smaller headlamps

The interior of the 103E was spartan in the extreme

On August 8, 1955, production was transferred from Dagenham to Doncaster (a plant acquired when Ford took over its body supplier, Briggs, in 1953). Changes were minimal: safety glass was adopted in 1956 and a 100E Anglia steering wheel was standardised in 1957. Remarkably, in 1953-4, more 103E Populars left Dagenham (66,933) than the combined total of the new 100E Anglias and Prefects (60,511).

Produced October 7, 1953 – September 1, 1959 (C741421 – C950078)

Specification as above except:
Engine in-line 1172cc four cylinder sv
Bore × stroke 63.5×92.56mm
Maximum power 30bhp @ 4000rpm
Transmission three speed
Chassis pressed steel channel
Wheelbase 90in (2286mm)
Track 45in (1143mm)
Length 143in (3632mm)
Suspension transverse leaf front/rear
Brakes four wheel mechanical
Bodywork Tudor, Fordor
Maximum speed (approx) 60mph (97km/h)
Total production (Britain) 148,020 BU, 7320 KD

GRAND TOTAL PRODUCTION 10HP: 580,564

Popular 10hp 103E 1953-59 Basically the old export Anglia, with a somewhat denuded specification – plastic-faced felt floor covering, single wiper, painted steel dashboard, silver-painted bumpers, body-colour hubcaps, smaller headlamps, no parcels shelf, ashtrays or interior light – the 103E was billed as the world's cheapest car, at a basic price of £390.

Consul/Zephyr Mk I
1950-56

Though history normally regards the 1949 US Ford range as the great turning point in the rebirth of the Ford Motor Company under Henry Ford II, there was nothing in the mechanical specification of that range that couldn't be matched by Ford's rivals, to whom hydraulic brakes and independent front suspension were old hat and the sidevalve V8 engine was the day before yesterday's news. In contrast the Consul/Zephyr range launched at the 1950 Olympia Motor Show by Ford of Britain was one of the most advanced designs of popular car then produced anywhere in the world, for it combined monocoque construction and an oversquare overhead valve engine (the first-ever use of upstairs valves by Ford) with the first application of an ingenious independent front suspension system designed by Ford's vice president of engineering, Earle MacPherson. Today, the MacPherson Strut is used by car makers all round the world. Another breakthrough for Ford was the use of 12V instead of 6V electrics, while the 13in wheels were the smallest seen on cars of that size in Britain up to then.

Because Ford of Britain's engineering

department was small, the new cars were designed in Dearborn, though engineers from Dagenham were sent there to work on the project. The oversquare engine dimensions were the first to be seen from a British manufacturer since the abolition of road tax based on cylinder bore in June 1947; indeed, the bore/stroke ratio was 0.96:1 at a time when the rival Vauxhall Velox had a bore/stroke ratio of 1.44:1. A couple of years later Vauxhall used identical dimensions for a new Velox engine . . .

Another instance of the advanced thinking applied to the Consul/Zephyr project was the pioneering use of au-

Consul Convertible
prototype

Mk I Consul
Convertible

Rear view of a
prototype Zephyr
Convertible, 1952

1953 Zephyr
Convertible

tomatic transfer machinery to produce the cylinder blocks, a move which doubled production rates at a stroke.

The Consul and Zephyr differed mainly in front end treatment and 4in extra wheelbase on the larger car to accommodate the extra two cylinders.

A redesigned instrument panel which incorporated a full-width parcel shelf was shown in prototype form at the October 1951 Motor Show. It was intended to replace the original "flat dash" – criticised for its lack of stowage space – though it was slow to get into production and the changeover was not fully accomplished until September 1952. Higher ratio final drive and slightly lower intermediate ratios were adopted in November 1951. In April 1953 the intermediate ratios reverted to the 1951 specification.

Initially, only four-door saloons were available but at the October 1951 Motor Show a prototype of a Zephyr Six two-door convertible was exhibited. The convertible (available on both Consul and Zephyr) was not put into full production until 1953, as problems were experienced with structural rigidity, and production convertibles, built by Carbodies of Coventry, needed a special "X"-form bracing welded beneath the floor to improve matters. An unusual feature of the design was a hood that

Consul Convertible with the hood in the "Coupe de Ville" position

Abbott estate conversion of the Mk I Zephyr

could be used in the "coupé de ville" position; the Zephyr Convertible's hood was electro-hydraulically operated.

Though it was built by an outside supplier, the convertible was classed as a production model since the body-shells were modified and trimmed in Coventry but returned to Dagenham for final assembly. Another variant on the theme was the "luggage locker expansion" launched at the 1954 Motor Show by E.D. Abbot of Farnham in which the roof was extended rearwards (the extra pressing was done with concrete dies instead of steel) and an extra pair of side windows added along with a side hinged rear door to create an estate car at modest extra cost (at its launch the price of the conversion was quoted at £145).

The performance capabilities of the Zephyr were shown when Dutchman Maurice Gatsonides won the 1953 Monte Carlo Rally with a virtually-standard car, modified only in the fitment of an adjustable-jet carburettor (and a switch in the brake-light circuit so that "Gatso" could delude competitors following closely on his tail into braking too late on bends!).

In October 1953 both the Consul and Zephyr were facelifted in minor details and a new de luxe variant on the Zephyr theme called the Zephyr Zodiac was

introduced. This featured "all the special fittings that the fonder owner loves" including two-tone paint and leather upholstery, gold-plated insignia, heater and demister, screen washer and whitewall tyres (though the radio was an extra): it also had a raised compression ratio which enabled the car to use premium-grade petrol and lifted power output from 68 to 71bhp.

But for the ultimate performance, keen owners fitted their Zephyrs with a Raymond Mays head; this most desirable accessory for the Zephyr featured triple SU carburettors and, with the optional overdrive, could boost top speed to over 100mph.

Convertible production: Consul 3749, Zephyr 4048.

Consul 1951-56

Produced January 1, 1951 (EOTA 001) – February 23, 1956 (EOTA 232198)

SPECIFICATION

Engine in-line ohv 1508cc four (EOTA)
Bore × stroke 79.37×76.2mm
Maximum power 47bhp @ 4400rpm
Transmission three speed
Chassis pressed steel monocoque
Wheelbase 100in (2540mm)
Track 50in (1270mm)
Length 166in (4215mm)
Suspension independent MacPherson strut front/semi-elliptic rear
Brakes four wheel hydraulic
Bodywork four door saloon, convertible, estate car
Maximum speed (approx) 75mph (120km/h)
Total production 231,481 (BU 158,012, KD 73,469)

Two-tone paint and gold-plated trim distinguished the Zephyr Zodiac

1953 Consul saloon with proposed extra brightwork ▼

Production Zephyr, 1953 ▼

Maurice Gatsonides won the 1953 Monte Carlo Rally with this Zephyr

Zephyr/Zephyr Zodiac 1951-56

Produced February 12, 1951 (EOTA 0001) – February 23, 1956 (EOTTA 175807). First Zephyr Zodiac November 2, 1953 (EOTTA 64273)

Specification as above except:
Wheelbase 104in (2640mm)
Length 172in (4369mm)
Engine 2262cc six cylinder (EOTTA)
Maximum power 68bhp @ 4000rpm (Zodiac 71bhp @ 4200rpm)
Maximum speed (approx) 85mph (137km/h)
Total production Zephyr Six 152,677, Zephyr Zodiac 22,634.
Grand total production: 175,311 (BU 98,386 KD 76,925)

Introduction of 100E Anglia and Prefect at the 1953 Motor Show

1954 100E Anglia

Luggage accommodation of the 1953 100E Anglia: note the early rear lamp pattern

Simple dash layout of the 100E Angia ◄

1957 Anglia facelift with "lattice" grille

The 1953 100E Prefect

Rear view of the 100E Prefect shows the larger lamps fitted from 1957 ▼

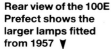

"Spacious and well-furnished" passenger compartment of the 100E Prefect ▼

100E and its derivatives
1953-62

Anglia/Prefect 1953-59 The introduction of the 100E range at the 1953 Motor Show was a major step forward for Ford, for these were Ford's first monocoque construction small cars, the more austere Anglia being available only in two- and the better-equipped Prefect in four-door form. Experimental overhead valve engines had been built, but this thoroughly modern small car surprised the pundits by having a flathead engine. Though the sidevalve power unit retained the traditional 1172cc capacity and the same bore and stroke as its predecessor, it was in fact a completely new engine with a different cylinder block and head, crankshaft, adjustable tappets ... nothing was the same apart from those crucial dimensions, which allowed existing production machinery to be used as a cost-saving measure. The new design, smoother-running than its predecessor, still had that typical sidevalve engine note, which gives the 100E a considerable period charm. The MacPherson strut suspension wrought miracles with the handling, and 100Es were both raced and rallied to good effect.

The first minor modifications came at the October 1954 Motor Show – twin wipers and a lockable boot on the Anglia, ashtrays and winding windows for rear-seat passengers on the Prefect. Early in 1955, lower indirect gears were standardised. In October 1955 both cars were face-lifted, the main changes being a new instrument panel layout and separate rear flashing indicators. De Luxe versions also appeared at the same time, with extra external chrome trim and two-tone interiors: basic models were made more so . . .

A more noticeable facelift took place in October 1957, when a new mesh grille arrived for the Anglia, and for both ranges "textured headlight mouldings", larger rear windows, redesigned taillight cluster and a new instrument panel; the De Luxe models gained a lockable glove box instead of the parcels shelf. The option of a NewtonDrive semi-automatic transmission with centrifugal clutch was offered, but there were few takers and it was withdrawn in 1958; total production of NewtonDrive-equipped 100Es is believed to number only 50 cars.

Anglia produced October 28, 1953 (100E 0001) – September 4, 1959 (100E 784685)
Prefect produced December 17, 1953 (100E 10170) – September 15, 1959 (100E 787684)

SPECIFICATION

Engine in-line 1172cc four cylinder sv
Bore × stroke 63.5×92.5mm
Maximum power 36bhp @ 4500rpm
Transmission three speed
Chassis pressed steel monocoque
Suspension independent MacPherson strut front/semi-elliptic rear
Wheelbase 87in (2210mm)
Track 48in (1220mm)
Length 151.25in (3840mm)
Brakes four wheel hydraulic
Bodywork two door (Anglia), four door (Prefect) saloon
Maximum speed (approx) 70mph (112km/h)
Total production Anglia 279,203 BU, 66,638 KD; Prefect 178,750 BU, 76,905 KD

Original version of the 100E Squire Estate, 1956

Escort/Squire 1955-61/1955-59 The first estate car actually bodied at Dagenham, the Escort corresponded in essence to the Anglia De Luxe, while the better-equipped Squire was trimmed to Prefect level – though it was only a two-door – and had wood rubbing strakes along its side in deference to the old Ford "woodie" bodies. Rear doors were split horizontally. The Squire lost its external woodwork in the October 1957 facelift and the two model lines were merged into a single Escort model when the 100E saloons were discontinued in September 1959.

Escort produced September 13, 1955 – April 29, 1961
Squire produced September 23, 1955 – September 9, 1959

Specification as above
Total production Escort 30,976 BU, 2155 KD, Squire 15,952 BU, 1860 KD

The Escort Estate, 1957

The 1957 Squire did away with the wooden side strakes

The 107E Prefect was a continuation of the 100E with the 997cc Anglia engine and gearbox

1959 Popular De Luxe

Popular 1959-62 When the thoroughly modern 105E Anglia came out in 1959, the old 100E Anglia was downgraded to become the new Popular; externally it differed only in having simpler round rear lamps. The Standard Popular had no parcel shelf or opening quarter lights, fittings found only on the De Luxe version.

Produced August 25, 1959 (100E 784686) – June 1962 (B115380)

Specification as above
Total production 120,815 BU, 5300 KD

GRAND TOTAL PRODUCTION 100E: 778,554

Prefect 107E 1959-61 Because the new Anglia 105E was only available in two-door form, the old Prefect 100E bodyshell was continued to retain a low-priced four-door model, but with the new 105E power unit and four-speed transmission. Only available to De Luxe specification, it had a two-tone paint scheme, floor carpets front and rear and redesigned seats.

Produced May 5, 1959 – June 1961

Specification as above except:
Engine in-line 997cc four cylinder ohv
Bore × stroke 80.96×48.41mm
Maximum power 39bhp @ 5000rpm
Transmission four speed
Maximum speed 73mph (117km/h)
Total production 38,154 (27,314 BU, 10,840 KD)

The 1959 Popular was a continuation of the Anglia

An early Mk II Zodiac saloon, 1956

1956 Consul Saloon at Finchingield, Essex ▼

Early production Mk II Zephyr, 1956 ▼

The Mk II Consul Convertible

Consul/Zephyr/Zodiac Mk II   1956-62

Though the Mk II Consul/Zephyr/ Zodiac range – marketed under the slogan "the Three Graces" – followed the general design principles of the Mk I line, the new cars had very few components in common with their predecessors. The new bodyshells were more commodious, and wheelbase and track were increased; but though the front and rear end treatment of each model was different, the centre section "greenhouse' was identical apart from trim. The body monocoque was some 12.5 per cent better in terms of torsional and beam stiffness than the Mk I shell. A semi-wraparound windscreen was specified.

The engines were redesigned to give an increase of .125in in both bore and stroke, equivalent to a 12.5 per cent greater swept volume; other improvements included hollow-cast crankshafts, larger main and big end bearings and a new cylinder head with inclined valves in a squish-type combustion chamber. The intention behind the new power units was to enable a higher final drive ratio to be used, giving a similar performance to the Mk I at lower rpm. Borg-Warner overdrive was optional on all models

from the start of production and brakes were larger to cope with the increase in power.

Convertible versions of Consul and Zephyr were also included in the range from the launch; convertibles were always rare, representing some 2.4 per cent (16,309 units) of total production but were included in the range because Ford-Britain's new chairman Sir Patrick Hennessy liked them (and would indeed keep his Mk II Zodiac convertible long into his retirement; the car survives in the hands of a West London en-

thusiast). A "first" for the British car industry was the fitment of a combined key-operated ignition/starter switch.

The more luxurious Zodiac had a heater as standard and elaborate rear-end decoration in the shape of a "washboard panel finished in gold" which added a couple of inches to the overall length. Gold-plated badges, a special grille and two-tone paint were other distinguishing features of this top-of-the-range model. At the October 1956 Motor Show, a Zodiac convertible made its debut, a PVC lining and stan-

1958 "Low Line" Zodiac

1959 Zephyr Convertible: note chromed headlamp rims

Dashboard of "Low Line" Consul ▼

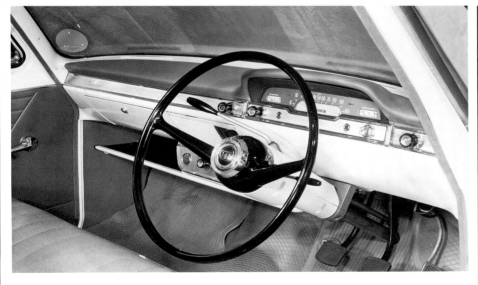

introduction of the "Low Line" from Consul 204E 166611 and Zephyr 206E 152231. A new roof pressing reduced the overall height of the cars by some 1.5in, while stainless steel gutter and windscreen and rear window surrounds, chromed headlamp bezels and new rear lamps for Consul and Zephyr were other external improvements. Other changes extolled by the Ford publicists were: "new, spring-gay colours [to] enhance that 'fine-car' finish – and then look inside! *Everything's new!* Facia panel, controls, steering column shroud, door trims, seating design and materials are all completely – and supremely elegantly – restyled to make your motoring more pleasurable, more practical than ever before."

The dashboard restyling included the addition of "a cowl formed in shock-absorbent material" and standard sunvisors in "a soft, padded plastic material with collapsible frames", both indicative of the increased emphasis on safety features in the redesign of the range., Standard upholstery was in "Cougar Grain" PVC, heralded as "a departure from the traditional practice of using synthetic materials to imitate cow hide". Also new was a "twist-to-release" handbrake and a half-horn ring for all models except the Consul, which had a push-button on the steering wheel hub. All the improve-

dard power operation differentiating its hood from the other Ford convertibles; Borg-Warner automatic transmission became an optional extra for Zephyr and Zodiac while Abbott of Farnham unveiled an estate conversion for Consul, Zephyr and Zodiac. Like the MkI "Farnham", it consisted of an extended roof, new side panels incorporating windows aft of the rear doors and a single rear door.

At that period, Ford Australia was manufacturing British Fords from KD kits and for that market a pick-up Mk II

was built at Dagenham from November 1956, mostly in KD form although 46 built-up pick-ups were also shipped.

A Consul De Luxe was added to the range in October 1957 with two-tone paintwork and appointments almost to Zodiac standard (though the heater was still an option). At the same time a new grille design was adopted for the Zephyr, with horizontal bars in a "triptych" layout replacing the old "eggcrate" pattern.

The major facelift for the Mk II range occurred in February 1959, with the

**Facelifted Mk II
Abbott Estate,
October 1959**

**1960 Zephyr saloon
with Allard sunroof
conversion**

ments were carried out without any increase in price.

A major step forward was the introduction in September 1960 of optional power-assisted front disc brakes on all models, making the Consul the cheapest British car with front discs; Ford dealers offered a retro-fit disc brake conversion for earlier cars. In fact discs had been seen on rallying Mk IIs since 1958 and some rally cars even had discs all round. The disc brake option proved so popular that from May 1961 front discs were standardised across the range, as were sealed-beam headlamps. At the same time the model name scripts were deleted from the rear fins and the Consul became known as the "Consul 375" to differentiate it from the newly launched "Consul Classic 315", Dagenham management at that time wanting to use the "Consul" name as an identification for all its medium-size saloons (which is why there was no "Consul" model in the new large car range which was at an advanced stage of development at Dagenham).

MkII convertible production
Consul 9398, Zephyr 5139, Zodiac 1772.

Consul 1956-62

Produced
Saloon February 6, 1956 – April 1962
Estate October 1956 – February 1962 (KD March 1959 – January 1961)
Pick-up November 1956 – August 1959 (KD June 1957 – January 1961)

SPECIFICATION

Engine in-line 1703cc ohv four cylinder (204E)
Bore × stroke 82.55×79.5mm
Maximum power 59bhp @ 4400rpm
Transmission three speed manual (automatic optional)
Chassis pressed steel monocoque
Wheelbase 104.5in (2655mm)
Track 53in (1346mm)
Length 173.77in (4414mm)
Suspension independent MacPherson strut front/semi-elliptic rear
Brakes four wheel hydraulic
Bodywork four door saloon, convertible, estate car.
Maximum speed (approx) 80mph (129km/h)
Total production 380,983 (Saloon: 290,951 BU, 59,293 KD; Estate Car*: 5643 BU, KD Australian station wagon* 7470; Pick-up*: 46 BU, KD Australian Utility* 17,580)
(* combined 4- and 6-cylinder production)

Zephyr/Zodiac 1956-62

Specification as above except:
Engine 2553cc ohv six (206E) cylinder ohv
Maximum power 85bhp @ 4400rpm
Wheelbase 107in (2718mm)
Length Zephyr 178.5in (4534mm); Zodiac 180.5in (4585mm)
Maximum speed (approx) 85mph (137km/h)
Total production 301,417 (177,585 BU, 123,852 KD)

Produced January 19, 1956 – April 1962

Classic 1961-63

Though its styling looked American, the Classic – with its Lincoln-inspired rear window – was "styled at Dagenham by Dagenham people"; launched in May 1961 it was intended to fill the gap between Anglia and Consul and to move the Ford image perceptively up-market. It was also not intended for a long production life, for the Cortina was already in an advanced state of development when the Classic (or "Consul Classic 315" to give it its full name) was introduced in mid-May 1961. Indeed as a former Ford engineer recalls, the Classic's pressings were made on short-life Kirksite dies and little attempt had been made to save weight in the body structure.

The 1340cc engine used the same block, valves, springs and pistons as the 105E Anglia but the stroke was increased to 65.07mm; the four-speed transmission was the same as the Anglia's, but offered the option of a column gearshift in addition to the floor change. The Classic also used the same clutch (but with stronger springs and new centre) and hypoid rear axle, though larger tyres gave a speed of 16.47mph/1000rpm against the Anglia's 16.09mph.

Though Ford engineers had ex-

The Classic was a pioneer of the quad headlamp look

Side elevation of the two-door Classic, 1963

perimented with independent rear suspension during the development of the Classic, they decided that "a simple irs design would be inferior to the live axle and leaf spring arrangement adopted". The Classic pioneered quadruple headlamps on family cars and the lighting was said by the press "to be good enough for a much faster car".

A notable feature of the design was the size of the boot, said to be "quite the largest on any medium-sized car yet produced", a feature emphasised by Ford publicists, who photographed a girl sitting in a deckchair in the open boot . . . Disc brakes were standardised, though servo assistance was not fitted.

The De Luxe versions had extra bright-metal interior and exterior trim, including a five-star motif across the radiator grille, combined door pulls and armrests, two-tone PVC upholstery (combination hide and PVC was extra)

optional steering column change, floor carpet, passenger sun vizor, rear ashtray and cigar lighter, windscreen washer, headlamp flasher, twin horns, coat hooks and front door courtesy light. Heater and demister and whitewall tyres were extras.

The robust construction of the Classic had resulted in a kerb weight of 2095lb and that, coupled with the relatively high final drive ratio ("to meet the requirements of Continental and American markets") led to complaints that the engine lacked flexibility. So in August 1962 Ford unveiled a new version of the Classic with a 1500cc engine; the new power unit had five main bearings instead of three, offered 10 per cent more torque and raised top speed by some 3mph. the crankshaft was now solid rather than cored-out, since "Ford engineers now admit that the advantages of a cored-out crankshaft are more

Dashboard of Classic

Classic had 21 cu.ft. of boot space

theoretical than real". Another improvement was that the gearbox had synchromesh on all four speeds.

Road testers appreciated "the light and precise steering . . . particularly on a windy day, for the car is decidedly affected by gusty side winds and needs frequent steering correction". The rear end of the Classic also exhibited a tendency to break away when the car was lightly loaded: "this trait is easy to counteract, however, because of the responsive steering". But by now the advent of the Cortina had rendered the Classic rather superfluous and only 27,000 of the new model had been produced by the time production ended just over a year later.

Classic 1340cc   1961-62

Produced
Standard two-door June 1961 – August 1962
Standard four-door April 1961 – July 1962
De Luxe two-door April 1961 – July 1962
De Luxe four-door April 1961 – August 1962

SPECIFICATION

Engine in-line 1340cc four cylinder ohv
Bore × stroke 80.96×65.07mm
Maximum power 56.5bhp @ 5000rpm
Transmission four speed
Chassis pressed steel monocoque

Suspension independent MacPherson strut front/semi-elliptic rear
Wheelbase 99in (2515mm)
Track 49.5in (1257mm)
Length 170.8in (4338mm)
Brakes four wheel hydraulic (front disc/rear drum)
Bodywork four door saloon
Maximum speed (approx) 78mph (126km/h)
Total production 84,694 (Standard two-door 4185, Standard four-door 6124, De Luxe two-door 18,197, De Luxe four-door 56,188)

Classic 1500cc   1962-63

Produced July 28, 1962 – September 1963

Specification as above except:
Engine in-line 1500cc four cylinder ohv
Bore × stroke 80.97×72.82mm
Maximum power 59.5bhp @ 4600rpm
Maximum speed (approx) 82mph (132km/h)
Total production 24,531 BU, 2000 KD (Standard two-door 840, Standard four-door 1770, De Luxe two-door 6742, De Luxe four-door 17,179)

Capri   1961-64

The first European Ford to bear the name "Capri" (originally used on an American Lincoln model), the Consul Capri 335 was aimed squarely at the export market and the first few weeks' production was for overseas sale only. The Capri made its show debut at the September 1961 Frankfurt Automobil-Ausstellung on a stand full of Ford-Germany Taunuses: "The only British Ford shown, it had all the others licked for looks," commented *The Autocar*. On the opening day, 86 Capris were sold and the marketing men were talking optimistically of sales of 2000 during 1962.

In fact, from the waist down, the Capri was identical to the two-door Classic apart from minor changes to the doors to accommodate a different type of window winding mechanism. The tremendous difference in appearance was achieved by replacing the saloon "greenhouse" with a steamlined coupé top, whose rear window was raked at 40 deg from the horizontal; the lower roof line reduced overall height by 2in.

The Capri had better front seats (trimmed in two-tone PVC as standard or optionally in leather) than the Classic, but only nominal rear seats in the shape of a thinly padded shelf more suited to the

1962 Capri 109E ▲

1963 Capri 116E with 1500cc engine ▼

carriage of luggage since there was restricted headroom; cushions to cover this platform were optional extras which only slightly mitigated the "mediocre comfort" complained of by road testers. The semi-elliptic rear side windows gave a foretaste of the style that was to distinguish a later car called Capri and wound down flush with the rear sill to create a pillarless coupé.

Other interior trim differences giving the Capri the edge over the Classic were a fitted nylon carpet and "white sequinned PVC" headlining. Driving controls and instruments were identical to those of the Classic but the steering wheel was lowered by 0.5in. The reduced top-hamper, it seems, improved the handling compared with the Classic, for road-testers spoke approvingly of its safe and predictable handling ("when cornering very fast in the dry it was almost impossible to make the tyres lose adhesion") and remarked that the Capri "is not much affected by cross-winds". In common with the Classic, the Capri gained the new 1500cc power unit in July 1962 to counteract criticism of poor low-speed flexibility.

On February 21, 1963, a new performance variant of the Capri, the GT, was unveiled, in response to an "important movement to get more fun into motoring, more liveliness, more perfor-

mance". Modifications to the engine – particularly the fitting of a twin-choke Weber carburettor, four-branch exhaust, larger exhaust valves and a Keith Duckworth-designed high-lift camshaft – raised power by over 30 per cent, torque by 12 per cent and increased the useful rev band by 500rpm. A remote-control floor shift was fitted and a supplementary instrument panel carried rev counter, ammeter and oil pressure gauge. The front discs were now servo assisted so that a harder pad

material could be used. At only £115 more than the standard model, the Capri GT offered excellent value for money and remained in production after the standard Capri had been withdrawn, though the final year's sales of only 412 units hardly seemed worth the effort.

In 1962 the London coachbuilders Hooper's Motor Services announced a customised version of the Capri, with 12-18 coats of cellulose to customer choice, a plain chrome strip replacing

The 1959 105E Anglia with optional two-tone paintwork

the five star motif in the radiator grille, a painted back panel, new rear lamp clusters, front and rear overriders, a chrome exhaust sleeve and a chrome grip on the rear number plate (which hinged down to reveal the petrol filler) and a completely redesigned interior with Connolly leather trim and wood veneer fascia panel. The standard front seats were replaced by fully-reclining bucket seats and two small bucket seats were fitted in the rear compartment. Only a handful of these Hooper Capris was built.

Capri 1340cc 1961-62

Produced July 1961 – August 1962

SPECIFICATION

Engine in-line 1340cc four cylinder ohv
Bore × stroke 80.96×65.07mm
Maximum power 56.5bhp @ 5000rpm
Transmission four speed
Chassis pressed steel monocoque
Suspension independent MacPherson strut front/semi-elliptic rear
Wheelbase 99in (2515mm)
Track 49.5in (1257mm)
Length 170.8in (4338mm)
Brakes four wheel hydraulic, front disc/rear drum
Bodywork two door coupé

Maximum speed (approx) 82.5mph (133km/h)
Total production 11,143 (9852 BU, 1291 KD)

Capri 1500cc 1962-64

Produced July 28, 1962 – September 1963 (Capri GT February 1963 – July 1964)

Specification as above except:
Engine in-line 1500cc four cylinder ohv
Bore × stroke 80.97×72.82mm
Standard 1500 engine as Classic
GT Maximum power 78bhp @ 5200rpm
Maximum speed (approx) 95mph (153km/h)
Total production 6868 BU, 705 KD (Capri 5571; Capri GT 2002)

Anglia 105E and its derivatives 1959-67

In 1956 Ford of Britain opened its first research & development centre, in a former glass works in Birmingham – since the Midlands was then the centre of the British motor industry and skilled motor engineers could more easily be found there. It built several concept cars, but only one of these found its way into production: as redesigned for mass-production by Fred Hart's Dagenham engineering team, this became the 105E Anglia and represented a complete break with Ford engineering tradition. For a start, it had a remarkably tough over-square, overhead valve power unit – its stroke/bore ratio of 0.6:1 was the lowest of any current production car. With a hollow cast crankshaft and capable of operating safely at high revolutions, the new power unit quickly became the preferred engine for Formula Junior racing. The new Anglia also had a four-speed transmission, something only previously found on Ford trucks; only the upper three ratios had synchromesh.

Novel, too, was the styling, given its final form by visiting American designer Elwood Engel and the subject of much wind-tunnel testing; the reverse rake

Journalists John Bolster and Raymond Baxter test the new Anglia

1963 Anglia Super: note wheel trims and twin bodyside chrome strips

rear window was a new idea for Britain, though it had previously appeared on the 1958 Lincoln Continental in the US. Its advantages were that it kept clear in bad weather and gave the rear passengers more headroom. Another aid to visibility was the use of electric screen wipers – a first for any British Ford.

The high-revving nature of the new power unit (first of a family that was to run to some 10 million engines) caught out drivers accustomed to the leisurely ways of the old sidevalve units with their ample bottom end torque; *Autocar* complained that "below 20mph in top gear the engine is decidedly lumpy". This led to carburettor modifications in January 1960. Like the contemporary Consul, the Anglia had recirculating ball steering, which tended to be vague in the straight-ahead position and over-light at all times, but the car's ride and handling were well-liked by road-testers. The Anglia's claim to be the "the world's most exciting light car" was rather mitigated by the almost simultaneous appearance of the new BMC Mini – but the Anglia was the only one of the two to bring its makers profits.

The Anglia was launched in standard and De Luxe versions, but the main differences between the two were mainly cosmetic and the heater was extra on both ranges. The De Luxe could be

Basic Anglia had narrow, painted grille

ordered with two-tone paint at extra cost and this was the first Ford model for which an automatic painting plant was considered (but didn't get past the prototype stage).

An important addition to the range were Standard and De Luxe estate cars, launched in September 1961: identical to the saloons up to the "B" pillar, they differed mechanically only in having stiffer rear springs and a lower final drive ratio.

At the beginning of September 1962, a "high-performance, luxury version" of the Anglia fitted with a new 1200cc engine was unveiled. It also had synchromesh on all four gears, wider brake drums (though the diameter was unchanged at 8in, there was 25 per cent more swept area) and higher bottom and reverse gearing. External dif-

ferences were a contrast-painted side stripe and roof panel; internally, the Super had pleated pvc upholstery, a loop-cord carpet instead of rubber, padded dashboard, twin horns, screen washer and cigarette lighter. The heater was standardised.

The larger engine could be specified on the cheaper Anglia models; this created some rare variants, like the 1200cc Standard saloon, of which just 43 were sold on the home market (but 7030 exported) and the 1200cc Standard estate, of which 51 out of a total production of only 215 were sold in Britain. Interestingly enough, the new Anglia Super was announced a fortnight before the real raison d'être for the 1200cc engine, the Cortina, was revealed.

Anglia production was transferred to

1965 Anglia estate

1966 version of the Anglia De Luxe

the new Merseyside factory at Halewood in March 1963. Changes from then on were largely cosmetic, though from October 1964 the option of a built-in radio was offered and built-in seat belt mounting points were standard. In 1965, the estate car gearing was standardised on saloons, too, with the old, higher, final drive ratio now the option. From 1966 a Ford carburettor replaced the earlier Solex or Lucas fitments. Metallic paint – venetian gold or blue mink – was available on the Super during the last year of production.

Produced September 3, 1959 – November 1967

SPECIFICATION

Engine in-line 997cc four cylinder ohv
Bore × stroke 80.96×48.41mm
Maximum power 39bhp @ 5000rpm
Transmission four speed
Chassis pressed steel monocoque
Suspension independent MacPherson strut front/semi-elliptic rear
Wheelbase 90.25in (2292mm)
Track 46.25in (1175mm)
Length 153.75in (3905mm)
Brakes four wheel hydraulic
Bodywork two door/four door saloon, estate car
Maximum speed (approx) 75mph (120km/h)

Anglia 1200 and Super 123E
1962-67

Produced September 1962 – November 1967

Specifications as above except:
Engine in-line 1198cc four cylinder ohv
Bore × stroke 80.96×58.17mm
Maximum power 48.5bhp @ 4800rpm
Maximum speed 80mph (128km/h)

Total Anglia production 1,083,960 (122,242 Standard, 752,967 De Luxe, 79,223 Super, 6686 Standard Estate, 122,842 De Luxe Estate)

Zephyr/Zodiac Mk III 1962-66

When it came to planning a replacement for the Mk II Consul/Zephyr/Zodiac range, Ford decided to move appreciably upmarket. First design thoughts – by Colin Neale (designer of the Mk II range) and visiting American stylist Elwood Engel – were rejected and Ford sought outside help from Frua of Turin. But the Frua design, too, was found wanting and the final form of the Mk III range took shape under the leadership of Dagenham's newly-appointed chief designer Roy Brown. (Canadian-born, Brown's best-known prior design had been the disastrous 1958 Edsel). Some of the elements of the Frua design – the roofline and rear quarters – were evident in the final version of the top-of-the-range Zodiac, which for the first time became a unique model and was the first of the new range to be announced, in a launch programme spread over a fortnight – which guaranteed the new big Fords star billing in three consecutive issues of the motoring weeklies.

The Zodiac was a six-light saloon and the first 100mph car to be catalogued by Dagenham, the increased performance due to a redesigned, higher-compression cylinder head and dual exhaust sys-

1964 Zephyr 4
saloon

1964 Zephyr 6
saloon

tem, (which by itself added 5.5bhp). With its mouth-organ grille incorporating quad headlamps, and more pronounced rear fins, the Zodiac looked bigger than its predecessor but was in fact almost exactly the same in overall dimensions; paradoxically, indeed, interior space was less generous due to the greater rake of the windscreen and a substantially lower roofline, and there were complaints about the lack of legroom in the back seats. However, there was more room from side to side due to the use of curved side windows, another feature taken from the Frua concept.

A major breakthrough was a four-speed all-synchromesh gearbox, the first such transmission to be used on a large Ford car (though the retention of a steering column gearshift was perhaps not so satisfactory); Borg-Warner manual overdrive or three-speed "no-maintenance fluid-drive automatic transmission" were available at extra cost. Two-speed electric windscreen wipers were another happy break with Ford tradition and screenwashers were standard on the Zodiac. The recirculating ball steering was of the new variable ratio type, lower-geared towards the extremities of lock to reduce parking effort. Another innovation was the use of zero-torque door locks, which could be closed without slamming. The foam

rubber seats were trimmed with Cirrus 500 PVC or Bedford cord with the option of hide trim.

Two weeks after the Zodiac, Ford unveiled the Zephyr 4 (which replaced the Mk II Consul) and the Zephyr 6 (replacing the Mk II Zephyr). Though they were basically the same mechanically as the more expensive model, they were four-light saloons with differently shaped rear door windows and a less steeply raked backlight, which was also less curved than that of the Zodiac. The Zephyrs also had simpler curved grilles and twin headlamps; the Zephyr 4 had a

narrower one-piece grille with the lamps on either side; the Zephyr 6 had a two-piece grille which extended to take in the lamp housings. There were fewer changes to the power units than on the Zodiac, though reciprocating parts were stronger and performance was noticeably brisker despite a slight increase in all-up weight. Standard trim was two-tone vinyl or "Saranweave", with hide trim available as an option.

On the eve of the October 1962 Motor Show came a substantial modification to the bodywork to provide a couple of inches' extra rear seat legroom; this in-

Appropriately-registered 1962 Zephyr 6 Police "Z-Car"

Tailgate of the Mk III Zephyr Estate was moulded from glass fibre

The Mk III Zodiac Estate was another ▼ Abbott conversion

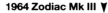

1964 Zodiac Mk III ▼

volved major modifications to the floor-pan, rear bulkhead and wheel arches plus a 1.75in increase in rear track which involved new halfshafts and axle casing. At the same time the interior trim of the Zephyr 4 was brought up to Zephyr 6 standard, with simulated wood fascia, horn ring and improved door trim.

Estate car conversions by Abbott of Farnham were also announced at the 1962 Motor Show and were available from mid-November; though the conversion had attractive lines, demand was low and only 4350 Mk III estates were built; all versions used the Zodiac body-shell because of its thin "C" pillar. The Mk III estate was a more thorough conversion than the two previous models, with a counterbalanced lift-up tailgate moulded from glass fibre and fitted with torsion-bar counterbalancing. The Zephyr 4 and 6 had the same tail trim while the Zodiac had four horizontal trim strips across the back panel and a full-width wraparound bumper. The same rear window as on the saloon versions was used.

At the same time, Hooper Motor Services announced a luxury treatment of the Zodiac along similar lines to their Capri conversion. A 14-coat cellulose paint job was allied to a complete retrim in Connolly hide and deep pile carpets,

plus a new polished veneer dash incorporating all the original instruments. The big stumbling block was the price of the basic car! Among the optional extras was a glass division.

At the 1963 Motor Show, improvements to the interior trim of the two Zephyrs were announced and all models now had simulated American walnut grain dashboards. More importantly, a floor gearshift was now available. Detail improvements to mechanical and trim details continued.

Then in January 1965 a new top-of-the-range Zodiac model was introduced which added a new word to the traditional Ford model designation lexicon: "Executive". The Zodiac Executive had such items as push-button Motorola radio, twin auxiliary lamps, seat belts, twin wing mirrors, locking petrol cap, high-output 30A dynamo and under-bonnet lamp as standard; trim was in black crushed hide and there was a choice of five colours, two the new acrylic metallic shades. *Autocar* complained of the Executive's "choppy ride" and still found the rear legroom "cramped", but concluded that while the Executive's performance and comfort were a little disappointing, "nonetheless it provides bulk and roominess with a prestige image somewhat above the ordinary run of the

mill". During the currency of the Mk III range, it received regular prime-time TV coverage as the "starring" vehicle in the popular BBC-TV police series "Z Cars".

Produced
Zephyr 4/6 January 1962 - January 1966
Zodiac December 1961 – January 1966
(Mk III estate cars introduced November 1962)

Zephyr 4 1962-66

SPECIFICATION

Engine in-line 1703cc four cylinder ohv
Bore × stroke 82.55×78.5mm
Maximum power 68bhp @ 4800rpm
Transmission four speed manual/optional overdrive or three speed automatic
Chassis pressed steel monocoque
Suspension independent MacPherson strut front/semi-elliptic rear
Brakes four wheel hydraulic; front discs/rear drums
Bodywork four door saloon, estate car
Length 180.5in (4585mm)
Track 53in (1346mm)
Wheelbase 107in (2718mm)
Maximum speed (approx) 84mph (135kph)
Total production 106,810 (Saloon BU 80,972, BU export 11,488, KD 13,625; Estate BU 663, BU export 62)

Cortina base model with painted grille

"Pre-Aeroflow" Cortina Super

Zephyr 6 1962-66

Specification as above except:
Engine in-line 2553cc six cylinder ohv
Maximum power 98bhp @ 4750rpm
Maximum speed (approx) 95mph (153kph)
Total production 107,380 (Saloon BU 43,512, BU export 15,891, KD 46,005; Estate BU 1632, BU export 340)

Zodiac 1961-66

Specification as above except:
Maximum power 109bhp @ 4800rpm
Maximum speed (approx) 103mph (166kph)
Total production (including Executive) 77,709 (Saloon BU 51,997, BU export 11,899, KD 12,160; Estate BU 1576, BU export 77)

Cortina Mk I and its derivatives 1962-66

Cortina Mk I 1962-66 Claimed to be the car that created a new segment in the popular car market – the so-called "C/D" class that bridged the gap between small and large family cars, the Mk I Cortina was in reality the embodiment of Ford-Britain chairman Sir Patrick Hennessy's desire not to be outdone by Ford-Germany, which was developing a new front-wheel drive model jointly with Ford-US under the codename "Cardinal" – a small North American bird. Sir Patrick's team wryly called their project "Archbishop" and set out to beat the Germans – though since Cologne had over a year's head start, a conventional mechanical layout was adopted to save time. Where the Archbishop scored was in its body design, the first application of aircraft stress calculations to a car monocoque; by eliminating unwanted metal, some 150lb was saved, equivalent to the weight of an extra passenger. Styling was by Roy Brown, lately responsible for the Ford-US Edsel.

The new model was launched on September 21, 1962, under the name "Cortina" (which was inspired by the venue of the 1960 Winter Olympics). Hen-

nessy's suggestion of "Caprino" was rejected when it was found to mean "goat dung" in Italian! Until September 1964 an additional "Consul" badge was carried on the bonnet.

The Cortina's principal rival was the new front-wheel driven BMC 1100 series – and here, too, the conventional Cortina scored heavily, for it was cheaper, larger, lighter and more capacious for identical performance; within a year of its launch, 250,000 Cortinas had been sold on the domestic and export markets – a record for a British car. However, on the British market, the 1100 was to remain the best seller until 1972.

Initially, only the 1200cc two-door Cortina was available; the four-door model followed during October 1962. In January 1963 came the 1500cc Cortina Super, with bigger (9in) brakes, improved trim and chrome strips on the body sides; a heater was standard equipment. At the same time Ford unveiled the limited production Lotus Cortina. Bodyshells were sent to the Lotus works at Cheshunt where they were fitted with Lotus twin-cam engines and light alloy door, bonnet and bootlid panels in true cottage industry style. Early models had Chapman's ingenious – but fatally frail – A-frame and coil spring rear suspension which had a tendency to cause catas-

Installing the twin-cam Lotus engine at Cheshunt

Lotus Cortina lifts a wheel

trophic oil leaks from the differential casing.

At the March 1963 Geneva Motor Show came Super and De Luxe estate cars, the cheaper De Luxe having the option of 1200cc or 1500cc power units. The 1500cc Super boasted Di-Noc simulated wood grain on its sides and rear. In April came the 1500cc "GT", with a Cosworth-designed camshaft for extra performance, front disc brakes and a remote-control gear change. From July grease nipples were no longer fitted. The instrument panel was redesigned in September 1963, with circular instruments in a binnacle above the steering column replacing the original ribbon speedometer; "silent shut" childproof locks were now fitted.

A major step forward came with the introduction of a Borg-Warner Type 35 automatic transmission as an £82 option on the Cortina 1500 in January 1964 (it was fitted to a handful of Lotus Cortinas for Ford management use but the fuel consumption was horrendous) but the real changes were reserved for the September introduction of the 1965 Cortina range, which was the first car fitted with Ford's revolutionary "Aeroflow" ventilation system; swivelling "eyeball" vents at either end of the dashboard gave full fresh-air ventilation without the need to open windows

Interior of the 1963 Lotus Cortina

1965 Lotus Cortinas for West Sussex police

1963 Cortina Super Estate

De Luxe Estate had Di-Noc "wood" panelling ▼

Cortina GT had 78bhp ▼

Peter Hughes drove a Cortina to outright victory in the 1964 East African Safari

(though the now-redundant front opening quarter lights were retained). The original two-spoke steering wheel was supplanted by a three-spoke design. A new close-mesh front grill incorporating the sidelights was an exterior sign of the changes, while front disc brakes were fitted across the range. Cortina was named "International Car of the Year 1964".

The 1966 Cortina range, announced in September 1965, saw the deletion of such items as the opening quarter lights, the Di-Noc external trim on the Super estate cars, the column gear shift and the Standard saloon. Lotus Cortinas swapped performance for reliability; the troublesome A-frame rear suspension was replaced by a conventional leaf-spring set-up and a close ratio gearbox was adopted.

On December 22, 1965, the 70mph overall speed limit was adopted "for a four month trial"; perversely, the Willment tuning firm chose that period to offer a limited edition GT, the "Super Sprint", with a 113mph top speed, but as the cost of the conversion took the car to around £1340 (a Lotus Cortina was £1007) it stood little chance.

Over 50 per cent of Mk I Cortinas were exported, home market sales totalling 489,884; this means that some models were rarely seen on British roads

and the rarest of these variants was the two-door Cortina 1500 Standard, of which just 347 were produced for the home market (and 19 complete cars and 1950 KD kits exported). Little more common at home and far rarer away was the four-door 1500 Standard, of which 535 were built for Britain, 55 complete cars and 520 kits being exported. Most numerous were the De Luxe 1200 saloons – 124,855 two-doors and 139,429 four-doors ("Tudors" and "Fordors" as they were known in an internal Ford parlance that went back to Model T days) for Britain alone, plus another 186,116 and 100,474 respectively for overseas markets.

Though it was conceived as a value-for-money package, the Mk I Cortina proved to be one of the most significant models in Ford's postwar history. Its sales success showed up the weaknesses of the British Motor Corporation and hastened its demise; it outsold its "in-house" rival, the "Cardinal" Taunus 12M; its performance derivatives established Ford as a major force in motorsport and added a much-needed touch of glamour to the corporate image. And though to modern drivers the Cortina may feel a trifle tall and narrow, in its day if offered a level of spaciousness that none of its rivals could match. No wonder the first owners to

Stirling Moss in his one-off two-door fastback Cortina

1966 Cortina De Luxe two door with Aeroflow ▼

Rear view of the 1966 Cortina showing Aeroflow extractor ▼ grilles on "C" pillar

take delivery of their new Cortinas in 1962 were so full of praise for its virtues: and the Cortina's legacy to the motor industry is the size of the C/D segment today, still accounting for about a quarter of new car sales.

Produced
1200cc September 1962 – November 1966
1500cc January 1963 – October 1966
Lotus Cortina launched January 1963
Estate cars launched March 1963
Cortina GT launched April 1963

Total production 1,013,391
Standard saloon 34,514, Deluxe saloon 704,871, Super saloon 77,753, 1500GT 76,947, Lotus Cortina 3301, Deluxe estate 108,219, Super estate 7786

Cortina 1200   1962-66

SPECIFICATION

Engine   in-line 1198cc four cylinder ohv
Bore × stroke   80.96×58.17mm
Maximum power   48.5bhp @ 4800rpm
Transmission   four speed
Chassis   pressed steel monocoque
Wheelbase   98.25in (2495mm)
Track   49.5in (1255mm)
Length   170.5in (4330mm)
Suspension   independent MacPherson strut front/semi-elliptic rear
Brakes   four wheel hydraulic

Bodywork   two door/four door saloon, estate car
Maximum speed (approx)   80mph (128km/h)

Cortina 1500   1963-66

Specification as above except:
Engine   in-line 1498cc four cylinder ohv
Bore × stroke   80.96×72.75mm
Maximum power   59.5bhp @ 4600rpm
Maximum speed (approx)   83mph (134km/h)

Cortina GT   1963-66

Specification as Cortina 1500 except:
Maximum power   78bhp @ 5200rpm
Maximum speed (approx)   91.5mph (147km/h)

Lotus Cortina   1963-66

Specification as above except:
Engine   in-line 1558cc four cylinder dohc
Bore × stroke   82.6×72.75mm
Maximum power   105bhp @ 5500rpm
Maximum speed (approx)   103mph (166km/h)

Corsair   1963-70

Announced on October 2, 1963, the Corsair was intended to replace the Classic (and early models were therefore badged "Consul Corsair") though press literature also eulogised that "it has almost the same feeling of roominess as the famous Mk II Consul", adding, somewhat confusingly, "it has . . . more headroom, more legroom at the rear and more bootspace".

Originally codenamed "Project Buccaneer", the Corsair was styled under the direction of Roy Brown, with John Fallis heading the exterior styling team; the front-end styling of the chosen design (eight different concepts were considered) was obviously inspired by the latest generation US Thunderbird. Great attention had been paid to soundproofing, with modifications being made to "tune" the drive train for quietness and double-skinned areas being installed in the floor pan. An unseen technological breakthrough was the first-ever application to a motor vehicle of printed-circuit electrics, with the instrumentation connected through a single master plug.

The Corsair was said to be the result of a two-year market survey across Europe, yet when it was launched in

both two- and four-door versions, there proved to be little demand for the two-door variants. The Corsair had column change as standard, with remote-control floor shift standard on the higher-performance GT version and optional on the De Luxe (or when bucket front seats were specified). The interior trim package was comprehensive – there was a choice of Cirrus 500 PVC "with metallic Knitweave" or Berkeley cloth on bench seats, plain Cirrus or Carlton cloth on bucket seats and the only extras on the De Luxe (which outsold the Standard in a ratio of 106 to 1!) were windscreen washer, two-tone trim, coat-hooks, courtesy light, package tray, two-tone horns operated by a horn ring and fitted carpets.

The Corsair was the first new model to be manufactured at the recently-opened Ford factory at Halewood on Merseyside; "much of Liverpool's prosperity stemmed indirectly from the Corsairs, the proud, swashbuckling pirates of the Barbary Coast who were relieved of their plunder by privateers with a government commission based on the Mersey", tortuously argued the press release. "Now the Consul Corsair, as proud and tough as its namesakes, will help to bring a different prosperity to Liverpool."

In October 1963 a Corsair driven by

Corsair two door

Eric Jackson and Ken Chambers circled the world in 43 days – a total of 29,991 land miles – and six months later a production model fitted with a 28 gallon tank lapped the Monza race circuit at an average of over 100mph for four days on end.

The in-line 1500cc engine was replaced in October 1965 by two new V4 power units of 1663cc and 1996cc, basically the same engines (but in a higher state of tune) as used in the new Transit van. "I've got a V in my bonnet" was the rather limp advertising slogan used to herald the change. Once again Ford was following the route of using the same block with crankshafts of different

throws to give the different swept volumes.

Unfortunately, the new power units were not the advance over the old engine that they promised to be: road-tested by *Autocar* the new 2000GT proved to be over 6mph slower than the old 1500GT, used more petrol and took an extra 2.5 sec to reach 80mph. Moreover, poor breathing characteristics gave the 2000GT almost exactly the same maximum speed as the normal Corsair 1700. The author recalls that the Corsair 1700 run by his office in 1968 became harsh and noisy at high speed, with pronounced body resonance over 80mph and a distressing tendency to oil plugs.

1966 Corsair V4 GT four door

1966 Corsair V4 Estate Car De Luxe

The Corsair driven round the world by Eric Jackson and Ken Chambers

The extra weight in the nose, allied to a lower steering ratio (4.7 turns lock-to-lock instead of 4) and recirculating-ball steering devoid of feel, made the car a pronounced – and occasionally alarming – understeerer . . .

Other changes allied to the introduction of the new power units were few: larger front brakes, a revised close-ratio gearbox on the GT, redesigned Mac-Pherson struts, new dashboards with improved instrumentation and comprehensive crash-padding just about sum it all up.

An estate car – converted by E. D. Abbott – was introduced on the Ford stand at the March 1966 Geneva Salon; aimed towards the luxury end of the estate car market, it had deep-pile carpet in its rear compartment. The lift-up tailgate

mated with the existing boot sill.

At the 1966 Motor Show, specialist convertors Crayford exhibited a convertible two-door Corsair; extra strengthening included a perimeter-type chassis, boxed rear wings, wider sills and a crossmember under the parcels shelf. Production is believed to have been minuscule.

In mainstream production, the GT was now optionally available with reclining bucket seats. Then, in January 1967, the Corsair 2000E was unveiled: a double-choke Weber carburettor and redesigned camshaft solved the breathing problems and the interior trim included individual reclining front seats and a walnut veneer dash. Though the 2000E was promoted as the successor to the GT, in fact production of the GT con-

tinued in penny numbers for export. In May 1967 a 2000E driven – again – by the indefatigable Chambers and Jackson arrived in London from Cape Town, having beaten the Union Castle Liner *Windsor Castle* by an hour, travelling 9752 miles against the liner's 7000 mile trip, at an average speed of 42mph.

An interesting "works" conversion which came to the public notice early in 1967 was a handful of estate cars fitted with 2.5 litre Zephyr V6 power units and used as service vehicles by the Ford rally team. In July 1969, right at the end of the Corsair's lifespan, production was transferred to Dagenham and the last 14,987 Corsairs were built in the Essex plant.

Produced

Two-door Standard September 1963 – September 1965
Four-door Standard July 1963 – August 1965
Two-door De Luxe August 1963 – September 1965
Four-door De Luxe June 1963 – September 1965
Two-Door GT August 1963 – September 1965
Four-door GT July 1963 – October 1965
2000cc V4 GT September 1965 – July 1969
V4 De Luxe September 1965 (1700cc)/ November 1966 (2000cc) – June 1970
Estate March 1966 – February 1968
2000E January 1967 – June 1970

1966 Corsair 2000E

1969 Corsair 2000 De Luxe

Corsair 1500   1963-65

SPECIFICATION

Engine in-line 1500cc four cylinder ohv
Bore × stroke 80.97×72.82mm
Maximum power 59.5bhp @ 4600rpm
Transmission four speed/automatic
Chassis pressed steel monocoque
Wheelbase 101in (2565mm)
Track 50in (1270mm)
Length 177in (4495mm)
Suspensioin independent MacPherson strut front/semi-elliptic rear
Brakes four wheel hydraulic, front disc/rear drum
Bodywork two- and four-door saloon, estate car
Maximum speed (approx) 84mph (135km/h)

1500GT   1963-65

Specification as above except:
Bodywork two- and four-door saloon
Maximum power 78bhp @ 5200rpm
Maximum speed (approx) 95mph (153km/h)

Corsair 1700   1965-68

Specification as above except:
Engine V4 1663cc ohv
Bore × stroke 93.66×60.35mm
Maximum power 76.5bhp @ 4750rpm
Transmission four speed/automatic
Maximum speed (approx) 84mph (135 km/h)

Corsair 2000   1965-70

As above except:
Engine V4 1996cc ohv
Bore × stroke 93.66×72.42mm
Maximum power 88bhp @ 4750rpm
Maximum speed (approx) 84mph (135 km/h)

Corsair 2000E   1967-70

Specification as above except:
Maximum power 102.5bhp @ 5000rpm
Maximum speed (approx) 98mph (158 km/h)

Total production Corsair 1500 159,951
Corsair Standard 1288 (Two-door 335, Four-door 953)
Corsair De Luxe 136,446 (Two-door 33,352, Four-door 103,094)
Corsair GT 21,857 (Two-door 6610, Four-door 15,247)

Total production Corsair V4 171,144
De Luxe Two-door 6450, Four-door 118,065
GT Two-door 1534, four-door 12,589
2000E 31566
Estate car 940

TOTAL CORSAIR PRODUCTION 331,095

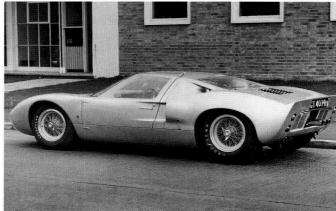

1967 GT40 Mk III

1965 GT40

GT40 1964-69

In the spring of 1963 Ford US nearly bought Ferrari but the deal fell through at the penultimate moment and Ford decided to set up its own racing unit to build a sports-racer that could win Le Mans. A small production facility was established in England because of the native expertise; the "Ford Advanced Vehicles" factory was at Slough, convenient for Heathrow Airport. Styled in Dearborn, the glass fibre bodywork of the new Ford GT car – derived from a mid-engined Lola – was moulded in England, where the chassis was also built by Abbey Panels of Coventry. The finished Ford GT stood just 40 inches high, so was soon christened "GT40".

Ford GTs with 4.2 litre V8 engines first ran at Le Mans in 1964 but none of the team finished (though Phil Hill did establish the fastest lap). The next GT40s had 4.7 litre engines.

From 1965 Carroll Shelby's Californian operation ran the racing programme, though the cars were still built in Slough. Some Shelby cars had longstroke 5.3 litre engines, but the big news of 1965 was the introduction of a new 7.0 litre GT40, the MkII.

For 1966, American-built "J" cars with bonded honeycomb chassis were added to the racing effort, but weren't ready for Le Mans, where a baker's dozen of assorted MkI and MkII Ford GTs was entered and three MkIIs finished 1-2-3 in line abreast.

On January 1, 1967, the Slough factory was taken over by JW Automotive Engineering, headed by John Wyer and John Willment. US-built Ford MkIV "J" cars won Le Mans in 1967, but at the end of the year Ford decided to withdraw from sports car endurance racing, having won most of the major events. However, Slough had been supplying road-going 4.7 litre GT40s to private customers since 1965 and in 1966 a road-equipped GT40 was sold to Grady Davis, a vice-president of Gulf Oil. See-

ing the publicity value of racing, Davis agreed that Gulf would back JW in the construction of three lightweight 5 litre GT40s known as "Mirages"; after a change in the rules had made them obsolete for 1968, two Mirages were rebuilt as lightweight GT40s and one of them – GT40 P/1075 – won the 1968 Le Mans 24 hour race, run in September because General De Gaulle, with a singular disregard for the important things in life, had called a national referendum during the traditional Le Mans weekend in June. P/1075 was victorious in 1969, too, the first car to win Le Mans twice. Road-going MkI and MkIII GT40s with fully trimmed interiors and luggage boxes in the engine compartment were

1966 Cortina Mk II four door

built, the MkIII – built only as a road car – having quad lamps and a central gear change instead of the right-hand lever of the MkI.

Produced 1 April 1964 (prototype) – 27 June 1969 (MkIII)

Production 133 (12 prototype Ford GTs, 87 production GT40, 3 Mirage, 7 MkIII GT40 plus 7 post-production cars, 5 cars built by Alan Mann Racing, 12 J Car chassis).

GT40 MkI

Engine 4735cc V8 ohv
Bore × stroke 101.6×72.9mm
Maximum power 380bhp @ 6500rpm
Transmission five speed
Chassis steel semi-monocoque
Wheelbase 95in (2413mm)
Track 55in (1397mm)
Length 164.5in (4178mm)
Suspension independent coil spring double wishbone front/independent coil spring upper and lower trailing arms with upper link and lower wishbone rear
Brakes four wheel discs
Bodywork two door coupé
Maximum speed (approx) 200mph (322km/h)

MKIII

Specification as above except:
Maximum power 306bhp @ 6000rpm

1967 Cortina Estate Car

Cortina Mk II and its Derivatives 1966-70

Launched at the October 1966 Earls Court Motor Show, the Mk II version of the Cortina was promoted as being "More Cortina". It used the same floor pan as its predecessor, but more interior room was given by the use of curved side windows, there was a new five-bearing 1300cc engine instead of the 1200cc unit and the front and rear track measurements were wider, with consequent improvement to the handling. Other mechanical changes included a diaphragm spring clutch (previously

only fitted to the GT), a Ford-built GPD carburettor instead of a Solex instrument and softer suspension settings (though body roll was reduced).

Among the available options were bench seats, column gearchange, automatic transmission on all versions except the GT, reclining front seats and radial ply tyres, with wide-rim 4½ J rims in addition on the GT. Cars intended for the American market had dual-circuit hydraulic brakes.

Base, De Luxe, Super and GT versions were available in both two- and four-door form from the start of production, with estate cars making their debut in February 1967. However, sporting enthusiasts had to wait until the next

In 1970, Ford loaned 30 1600E Cortinas to Britain's World Cup football team

The millionth export Cortina leaves Dagenham by an unorthodox route

Lotus Cortina 1967

March for the announcement of a new Lotus Cortina which was now built at Dagenham rather than at the new Lotus factory at Hethel, Norfolk (though production remained small). Also, the Special Equipment tune version of the Lotus-built engine – previously a costly extra – was standardised and the valve timing was modified following development by Ford engineers. The Corsair 2000E gearbox was standard on the new Lotus Cortina; a Lotus ultra-close ratio box was optional for competition work and a split propshaft was fitted instead of the single-piece shaft used on all other versions of the Mk II Cortina. But the dashboard and seats were almost the same as on the GT. A major change was that the Mk II Lotus Cortina was available in a full range of body colours and the traditional Lotus green sideflash was now only available as an extra on white cars.

From September 1967, crossflow cylinder heads were fitted to Cortina engines and a new 1600cc engine replaced the 1500cc unit; the new power units had 7.5 per cent (1300) and 15.5 per cent (1600) more power plus flatter torque curves. At the same time the Super gained the remote control gearshift as already fitted to the GT; radial-ply tyres were standardised on the GT and optional on De Luxe and Super. The Lotus Cortina became officially "Twin Cam" Cortina and gained a bootlid badge to prove it, plus leather-covered steering wheel, twin-tone horns, new central console, clock and leather gearstick gaiter. Very rare was a Lotus Cortina with the 16-valve FVA competition engine ("you can buy one if you have enough money and contacts").

A showtime surprise at Paris in October was the Cortina 1600E, a characterful "executive express" created by a group of enthusiastic product planners using the GT engine, Lotus suspension, wide-rimmed Rostyle sports wheels, a painted coachstripe and a luxury interior with a wooden dashboard. The vast majority of this very successful model were four-doors, though some two-door models were produced in left-hand drive form for the Continent (and a handful of rhd two-doors was created for Ford of Britain executives).

The year 1967 ended with the announcement that for the first time Cortina had topped the British sales charts. The extra weight of the Mk II Lotus Cortina had made it less and less competitive in rallies so in 1968 it was supplanted as the "works" car by the new Escort Twin Cam. From 1968 on there were few changes to the successful Mk II range, though remote gear shifts were standardised across the

The 1968 Cortina 1600E four door

Cortina 1600 GT four door

range in October 1968 and reclining seats became optional.

Produced September 1966 – September 1970

Estate cars launched February 1967
Lotus Cortina launched March 1968
Crossflow 1300/1600 engines launched September 1967
1600E launched October 1968

Total production 1,027,869
Standard saloon 14,324 2-door, 4914 4-door
Deluxe saloon 251,537 2-door, 347,462 4-door
Super saloon 18,950 2-door, 116,143 4-door
GT 62,592 2-door, 54,538 4-door
Lotus Cortina 4032
1600E 2-door 2563, 4-door 57,524
Estate car 90,290

Cortina 1300

SPECIFICATION

Engine in-line 1297cc four cylinder ohv
Bore × stroke 80.97×62.99mm
Maximum power 53.5bhp @ 5000rpm
Transmission four speed/automatic optional
Chassis pressed steel monocoque
Wheelbase 98in (2490mm)
Track 52.5in (1334mm)

Length 168in (4267mm)
Suspension independent MacPherson strut front/semi-elliptic rear
Brakes four wheel hydraulic, front disc/rear drum
Bodywork two door/four door saloon, estate car
Maximum speed (approx) 80mph (128km/h)

Cortina 1300 Crossflow

Specification as above except:
Maximum power 58bhp @ 5000rpm
Maximum speed (approx) 81mph (130km/h)

Cortina 1500

Specification as above except:
Engine in-line 1498cc four cylinder ohv
Bore × stroke 80.98×72.62
Maximum power 59.5bhp @ 4600rpm
Maximum speed (approx) 83mph (134km/h)

Cortina 1600 Crossflow

Specification as above except:
Engine in-line 1599cc four cylinder ohv
Bore × stroke 80.98×77.62
Maximum power 71bhp @ 5000rpm
Maximum speed (approx) 91mph (146km/h)

Cortina 1600 GT

Specification as above except:
Maximum power 88bhp @ 5400rpm
Maximum speed (approx) 100mph (161km/h)

Cortina Lotus

Specification as above except:
Engine in-line 1558cc four cylinder dohc
Bore × stroke 82.6×72.75mm
Maximum power 109.5bhp @ 6000rpm
Maximum speed (approx) 104mph (167km/h)

Zephyr/Zodiac Mk IV
1966-72

Development of the Mk IV Zephyr/Zodiac range began in mid-1961 under the code-name "Panda". The decision to use the new V-engine range created a problem for the designers because the short power unit naturally only needed a short engine compartment. Since the concept of European large cars called for a long bonnet, this gave unacceptable proportions until it was decided to house the spare wheel at an angle under the bonnet ahead of the radiator. Ford-Britain's new American director of engineering Harley Copp decreed that the new car should be larger than its predecessor, and the new car was therefore entirely different from the Mk III.

Of similar dimensions to the American Ford Fairlane, the Mk IV was launched on April 20, 1966, with V4 2 litre and V6 2.5 litre engines in the Zephyr and V6 3 litre in the Zodiac. Neat "bow-back" styling made the capacious boot look deceptively short, but the large expanse of bonnet was unkindly likened to the landing deck of an aircraft carrier by some journalists!

Copp had also insisted on independent rear suspension but the chosen design had many of the failings of swing-

Quad headlamps for the 1966 Zodiac Mk IV

The 1966 Zephyr 4 MkIV ◄

1966 Zephyr 4 Estate Car ▼

The 1966 Zodiac Executive

Full-width aluminium grille distinguished the 1968 Zephyr V6 De Luxe ►

Interior of 1966 Zodiac Executive ▼

axle suspension when the car was lightly laden. Coupled with the five turns lock-to-lock of the steering, this gave rise to alarming "tuck-under" of the outer rear wheel when cornering with the back seats empty.

The Mk IV range used the new Ford C4 automatic transmission or a new manual four-speed gearbox (which could be specified with a Laycock LH overdrive).

Zephyrs had a bench front seat and column change as standard and individual fixed-back front seats and floor shift as an option, while the Zodiac came as standard with individual reclining front seats and floor change, and the bench seat and column change were optional extras.

At the October 1966 Earls Court Show, Ford launched the Executive, based on the Zodiac and with the C4 transmission as standard. Hydrosteer power steering was fitted, enabling a slightly higher gearing to be used; the steering column was adjustable for rake. Crushed hide or "continental" nylon cloth upholstery could be specified, while deep pile carpet "completed the luxury feel on the inside". Externally, the Executive had a distinctive "Lincoln Star" radiator grille emblem, fog and driving lamps, name scripts fore and aft, a sunshine roof and wing mirrors.

**1972 Zodiac 3 litre
V6**

At the same time, E. D. Abbott unveiled their estate car conversions of the Zephyr and Zodiac, which were said to be the biggest estate cars built in Britain and had vinyl roofs as standard.

A number of changes was announced at the 1967 Motor Show: the new De Luxe Zephyrs and Zodiacs had a new radiator grille and "gunsight" bonnet ornament plus radial-ply tyres on 14in wheels as standard while the Zodiac gained power steering. Cars without power steering had a slightly lower ratio (six turns lock-to-lock!) to reduce steering effort and the camber angles for the rear suspension were revised to improve the roadholding. Zephyrs gained separate front seats as standard, trimmed in embossed Cirrus PVC, and reclining backrests were available as an extra. All de luxe models now had the central armrest locker previously only fitted on the Executive. From November 1967, the C4 transmission was replaced by the Borg-Warner Model 35, but reappeared on the 3 litre cars late in 1968.

The power units on the Zephyr/Zodiac range having proved liable to various problems associated with overheating, modifications were brought in during 1968. Another detail modification was the deletion of the remote radiator header tank – which had tended to crack at its mounting point – early in 1969.

For 1970, the springs were softened slightly and improved door seals lessened wind noise. The front seats on the De Luxe Zephyrs now offered better side support, heated rear windows were available as an option on all Zephyrs and were standard on Zodiac and Executive. Zodiacs now had an Executive type walnut dash; Executives now had walnut trim on the door cappings. Both lines gained bright metal side strakes and wheelarch cappings. But production of the Mk IV range had fallen almost without ceasing after the first full year, in which 50,593 cars were built; in 1970 the figure was only 18,925 and in the last year of manufacture, 1971, output was almost exactly one-third of the first year's figure.

**1971 Zodiac Estate
Car with ambulance
conversion**

Everyday Escort: the 1100 De Luxe had rubber mats and round headlamps

Extraordinary Escort: the RS1600 which Hannu Mikkola drove to victory in the 1972 East African Safari

Produced
Zephyr 4 December 1965 – December 1971
Zephyr 6 January 1966 – December 1971
Zodiac December 1965 – December 1971

Total production Zephyr 4 41,386 (BU 37,467, BU Exp 1901, KD 2018)
Zephyr 6 61,031 (BU 38,484, BU Exp 4748, KD 17,799)
Zodiac (includes Executive) 46,846 (BU 36,386, BU Exp 3599, KD 6861)

Zephyr 4   1965-71

SPECIFICATION

Engine 1996cc V4 ohv
Bore × stroke 93.7×72.4mm
Maximum power 112bhp @ 4750rpm
Transmission four speed manual/ optional overdrive or three speed automatic
Chassis pressed steel monocoque
Wheelbase 115in (2920mm)
Track 57in (1448mm)
Length 185.5in (4710mm)
Suspension independent MacPherson strut front/coil spring semi-trailing wishbone rear
Brakes four wheel discs
Bodywork four door saloon, estate car
Maximum speed (approx) 95mph (153km/h)

Zephyr 6   1966-71

Specification as above except:
Engine 2495cc V6 ohv
Bore × stroke 93.7×60.3mm
Maximum power 112bhp @ 4750rpm
Bodywork four door saloon, estate car
Maximum speed (approx) 102mph (164km/h)

Zodiac   1965-71

Specification as above except:
Engine 2993cc V6 ohv
Bore × stroke 93.7×72.4mm
Maximum power 136bhp @ 4750rpm
Bodywork four door saloon, estate car
Maximum speed (approx) 102mph (164km/h)

Escort Mk I and its derivatives   1968-74

"The small car that isn't" made its debut at the start of 1968. Originally developed as the "1968 Anglia", the Escort took on a wider role with the foundation of Ford of Europe in mid-1967 and became the first Ford model to be produced in Europe under the new organisation, being built at Saarlouis in Germany as well as at Halewood. Another "European" touch was that the all-synchromesh gearbox had been designed in Germany; a close-ratio version was fitted to the GT.

Detail planning for the new model had started in 1964 and had proceeded so well that in the two months between the start of production on Merseyside on November 17, 1967 and the official announcement on January 17, 1968, some 11,300 Escorts had been built and production was running at 500 cars a day. A prime distinguishing feature was the "dog-bone" grille (Ford stylists primly called it a "twin spatula" shape). Bodyshells had the sides pressed in one piece and initially only two-door Escorts were built. The redesigned front suspension had no anti-roll bar, a rear-angled compression strut locating the wheels (a conventional MacPherson lay-

Escort Super had carpets, square headlamps, chrome wheel arch trims

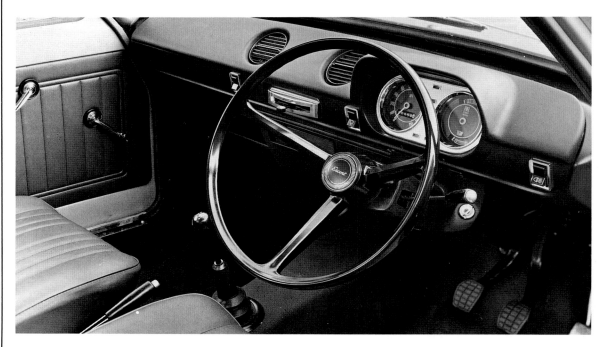

The controls of the 1968 Escort De Luxe

out with antiroll bar was adopted after a year). The Escort was the first Ford with rack-and-pinion steering.

Power units for the new model were completely revised versions of the "Kent" light car engine range (so-called because chief engine designer Alan Worters lived in Kent!) with five-bearing cranks and crossflow cylinder heads: the new 48bhp 1098cc version was used in the basic, De Luxe and 1100 Super Escorts, while the 1298cc unit appeared in the 1300 Super in 57bhp form and in the Escort GT with special cylinder head, high-lift camshaft, special inlet manifold and dual-choke Weber carburettor among the changes boosting power output to 72bhp.

Available right from the start was the high-performance Twin Cam – essentially the running gear of a Lotus Cortina in the 300lb lighter Escort bodyshell – with 165-13in wheels instead of the standard car's 12in units. Code-named "J25" (because the decision to proceed with the project had been made on January 25, 1967), the Twin Cam had come about because, seeing a prototype Escort being tested on the Boreham track where the Ford Competition Department was based, chief competition mechanic Bill Meade had thought "it would go like hell with a Twin Cam engine in it." The unofficial project was

Rear view of the Escort De Luxe

accepted for production and the first 25 cars were assembled at Boreham using the Type 48 bodyshell while every other "Twink" was built at Halewood, with its unique mechanicals fitted "off-line" into a specially-strengthened flared-arch Type 49 bodyshell. Group 3 homologation (parts for 500 cars made) was reached on March 1, 1968, with Group 2 homologation (parts for 1000 cars made) granted on May 1 the same year.

Of the other Escorts available at launch, the no-frills base model was intended principally as a fleet car and the cheapest "private" model in the range was the De Luxe, identifiable by its circular headlamps, rubber floor mats and

a spartan dash carrying just speedometer and fuel gauge (plus oil pressure/main beam/dynamo warning lights). The Super 1100 and 1300 had chrome strips round the wheel arches, carpets, better wheel trims, water temperature gauge and square headlamps. The GT was similar, with wider wheels and full instrumentation (including rev counter).

At the end of March, 1100 and 1300 Estates based on the De Luxe saloon appeared, with disc brakes standard on the larger car. An Escort Super Estate did not appear until May 1969 and in October 1969, four-door versions of the Escort range finally made their appear-

Escort 1300 GT

1970 Escort 1100L four door

Rear view of the Escort Estate showing one-pane rear windows

Escort 1300 De Luxe Estate Car

ance (legend has it that a "three-door" Escort was accidentally built early on combining sides from a two-door and four-door Escort).

The disruption to mainstream production caused by the building of the Twin Cam at Halewood led to the establishment of the Ford Advanced Vehicles Operation at Aveley in Essex in 1970 to hand-assemble high-performance versions of the Escort at a rate which at its peak approached 30 cars a day. The first "Aveley" Escort was the RS1600, a development of the Twin Cam with the new 16 valve Cosworth BDA twin cam engine; production of this model started at Halewood under the code-name "J26" in January 1970 before being transferred to Aveley that October. The "Twink" was only built at Halewood, ending in September 1970; sales faded away in the spring of 1971.

Alongside the RS1600, Aveley built the Mexico, based on the car which had won the 1970 World Cup Rally, which had an enlarged (1558cc) "Kent" push-rod engine for reliability. Additionally, three Mexico Estates were built and at least one escaped into private hands, as did a "one-off" Mexico motor caravan.

Also built at Aveley in its initial stages was the luxury Escort 1300E, launched in March 1973 and powered by the 1300GT engine, and with fitted pile car-

Escort Twin Cam had
Lotus Cortina engine

Escort Sport
1971-74

pet, "walnut" wood trim, halogen
auxiliary lamps and the choice of metallic purple, venetian gold or amber gold
metallic paint. Aveley built approx. 5000
of these before the model went "mainstream".

The final Escort model launched at
Aveley before falling sales caused by the
Middle East War forced its closure on
January 24, 1975, was the RS2000, with
an ohc 2 litre "Pinto" engine and a distinctive side decal. Launched in Britain
in October 1973, this model was also
built in lhd form at Saarlouis from June
1973. (Aveley-built Escorts should carry
a VIN code starting BFAT and have a
build date between October 1970 and
January 1975).

In October 1971 Ford had launched a
"mainstream" production performance
Escort, the Sport, which combined the
heavy-duty Type 49 bodyshell and 13in
wheels of the Mexico with the power-
train of the 1300GT. Production of the
1300E transferred to Halewood at the
end of 1973; a four-door version (mostly
for export) appeared in April 1974. Pre-
paration for the introduction of a Mk II
Escort had started with the introduction
of a revised floorpan fitted to the Mk I
from October 1973.

Produced October 1967 – December 1974

Total Halewood production 1,082,472
(2-door 611,305, 4-door 153,660, Estate

Escort RS1600 1970-
74

This one-off
Mexico motor
caravan was
decidedly unsafe

Escort 1300E 1973-74

Escort Mexico 1970-74

Distinctive livery of the RS2000 Escort

130,908, Van 186,599). Additionally 1263 J25 plus unknown total of J26 built.
AVO Escort production 1971-74 15,277 (RS1600 947, Mexico 9382, RS2000 4324 inc. Saarlouis production)

Escort 1100 1968-74

SPECIFICATION

Engine in-line 1098cc four cylinder ohv
Bore × stroke 81×53.3mm
Maximum power 48bhp @ 6000rpm
Transmission four speed
Chassis pressed steel monocoque
Wheelbase 94.5in (2400mm)
Track 50in (1270mm)
Length 157in (3988mm)
Suspension independent MacPherson strut front/semi-elliptic rear
Brakes four wheel hydraulic (front discs initially standard on 1300 estate and GT, optional on other models)
Bodywork two door/four door saloon, estate car
Maximum speed (approx) 80mph (129km/h)

Escort 1300 1968-74

Specification as above except:
Engine in-line 1298cc four-cylinder ohv
Bore × stroke 81×63mm
Maximum power 57bhp @ 5500rpm

Maximum speed (approx) 85mph (137km/h)

Escort 1300 GT/1300E 1968-74

Specification as above except:
Maximum power 72bhp @ 6000rpm
Maximum speed (approx) 99mph (159km/h)

Escort Twin Cam 1968-71

Specification as above except:
Engine in-line 1558cc four-cylinder dohc
Bore × stroke 82.55×72.75mm
Maximum power 106bhp @ 6000rpm
Maximum speed (approx) 113mph (182km/h)

Escort RS1600 1970-74

Specification as above except:
Engine in-line 1599cc BDA 16-valve dohc
Bore × stroke 80.97×77.62mm
Maximum power 120bhp @ 6500rpm
Maximum speed (approx) 113mph (182km/h)

Escort Mexico 1970-74

Specification as above except:
Engine in-line 1599cc four cylinder ohv
Bore × stroke 80.97×77.62rpm
Maximum power 86bhp @ 5500rpm
Maximum speed (approx) 108mph (174km/h)

Escort RS2000 1973-75

Specification as above except:
Engine in-line 1993cc four-cylinder ohv
Bore × stroke 90.82×76.95mm
Maximum power 100bhp @ 5750rpm
Maximum speed (approx) 108mph (174km/h)

Capri Mk I 1969-74

1969 Capri 1600 GT XLR with Rostyle wheels

1969 Capri 1600XL

"The car you've always promised yourself" went into production in November 1968 in Britain and Germany. The Capri 2+2 coupé was Europe's response to the market success of the 1964 Mustang in the United States. Early prototypes like "Colt" and "GBX" had many of the features of the production Capri (including the "hockey stick" side moulding) but rear seat visibility was a problem with the fastback styling. It was not until a Dunton designer created the elliptical side windows to lighten the heavy "C" pillars that the archetypal Mk I Capri was born.

Launched in January 1969, the Capri was offered in a confusing 26 basic derivatives combining various "custom plans" – the purely cosmetic Plan L for the exterior with chrome wheel, bodyside and exhaust trims and dummy air scoops (a locking petrol cap was the only item which performed a useful function!), the X "major interior kit" (reclining seats, dual horns and separate rear seats with a central armrest were included in this one) and Plan R for GT cars only, with sculptured road wheels, leather-rimmed steering wheel, flexible stalk map-reading light, halogen fog/driving lamps, matt black radiator grille

and a "special sports paint scheme in sub-gloss black" across bonnet, back panel and body sills. You could combine all the custom plans to make a Capri XLR for just £79 12s 10d!

The engine range consisted of 1300 and 1300GT, 1600 and 1600GT in-line fours and the 2000GT V4 (listed from the start, this didn't go into production until March 1969). Eight hand-built 1600GT Capris with 120bhp BDA twin-cam engines, glass fibre bonnets and Minilite wheels were seen at the press launch in Cyprus but failed to make production. Automatic transmission was optional for 1.6 and 2 litre Capris.

In September 1969 the 3000GT was

added to the range, its V6 engine modified to cope with higher cornering forces than it had been accustomed to in its alternative installation in Zodiacs. Distinguished by the "power bulge" in the bonnet, the Capri 3000GT and its luxury 3000E derivative (launched in March 1970) initially suffered from a wide-ratio Zodiac Mk IV gearbox but at the 1971 Motor Show improved 3000GT and 3000E models were launched as "the fastest production line cars ever to be sold by Ford in Britain". Improvements to the engine raised power output by 8 per cent to 138bhp; higher final drive and second gear ratios plus modified suspension and braking created a

1969 Capri 1600L

**Rear view of the
Capri Mk I in 1600GT
XLR guise**

Capri 2000 GT

**Capri 3000GT with
bonnet bulge arrived
in September 1969**

car that offered a similar level of performance (up to 120mph) to a £3000-plus E-Type Jaguar for half the price.

In November/December 1971 a 2 litre Capri Special was offered, painted Vista Orange, while another eyecatching derivative was the Capri S Special of May 1972. Offered in GT and XLR specification with 1.6, 2.0 and 3.0 litre engines, it was available in ebony black with red stripes or light emerald green with gold stripes. They heralded the introduction of the "power bulge" on smaller-engined models. This feature was standardised across the range in September 1972 and consequently had as much relevance to performance as

**Capri 2000GT
1972, now with quad
headlamps**

**British-built Capri
RS3100 boasted a
distinctive "duck-
tail" spoiler ▼**

the padding in a ballet dancer's tights . . .
More meaningful changes included better headlamps – bigger sealed-beam
units on square-lamp models and a
quad headlamp installation on the new
top-of-the-range Capri, the 3000GXL.
The suspension was modified – not
perhaps for the better – and the ohv
1600 unit was supplanted by the ohc
1600 as used in the Cortina Mk III in
72bhp single carb form or 88bhp twin-
carb GT tune. Out went the 1300GT engine; the British overhaul of the engine
lineup was less comprehensive than in
Germany, where the ohc Pinto design
was used exclusively from 1.3 to 3 litres.

Though the German-built road/race
Capri RS2600 was never sold in Britain,
when it came to developing its successor the work was carried out in Britain.
With a bored-out V6, four-headlamp
nose, quarter bumpers, alloy wheels
and a distinctive "duck-tail" spoiler, the
RS3100 went into production at
Halewood in November 1973. The timing could not have been worse, due to
the oil crisis. Moreover, the Capri line
was due to be replaced by a new Capri
codenamed "Diana" within a few
months and the RS3100 was only in production for three months. 248 were
sold.

**1972 Capri L had
revised lamp
treatment front and
rear and 1600s
gained the ohc
engine**

Capri RS2600 was Cologne built

A handful of Capri Convertibles was built by Crayford Conversions of Westerham, Kent

Produced November 1967 – December 1973

British production 374,700

Capri 1300 1969-74

SPECIFICATION

Engine in-line 1297cc four cylinder ohv
Bore × stroke 80.98×62.99mm
Maximum power 57bhp @ 5500rpm
Transmission four speed
Chassis pressed steel monocoque
Wheelbase 100.75in (2560mm)
Track 53in (1345mm)
Length 168in (4267mm)
Suspension independent MacPherson strut front/semi-elliptic rear
Brakes hydraulic, discs front/drums rear
Bodywork two door coupé
Maximum speed (approx) 86mph (138km/h)

Capri 1300GT 1969-71

Specification as above except:
Maximum power 72bhp @ 5500rpm
Maximum speed (approx) 94mph (151km/h)

Capri 1600 1969-72

Specification as above except:
Engine in-line 1593cc four cylinder ohv
Bore × stroke 87.65×66mm
Maximum power 72bhp @ 5500rpm
Transmission four speed/automatic optional
Maximum speed (approx) 93mph (153km/h)

Capri 1600GT 1969-72

Specification as above except:
Maximum power 88bhp @ 5700rpm
Maximum speed (approx) 100mph (161km/h)

Capri 1600 OHC 1972-73

Specification as above except:
Engine in-line 1593cc four cylinder ohc
Bore × stroke 87.65×66mm
Maximum power 88bhp @ 5700rpm
Maximum speed (approx) 101mph (162km/h)

Capri 2000GT 1969-73

Specification as above except:
Engine ohv 1996cc V4
Bore × stroke 93.66×72.41mm
Maximum power 92bhp @ 5250rpm
Maximum speed (approx) 108mph (174km/h)

Capri 3000GT 1969-73

Specification as above except:
Engine ohv 2994cc V6
Maximum power 128bhp @ 4750rpm. From 1971 138bhp @ 5300rpm
Maximum speed (approx) 120mph (193km/h)

Capri RS3100 1973

Specification as above except:
Engine ohv 3091cc V6
Bore × stroke 95.2×72.4mm
Maximum power 148bhp @ 5200rpm
Maximum speed (approx) 124mph (200km/h)

Cortina Mk III   1970-76

Developed under the leadership of self-opinionated American chief engineer Harley Copp, the Mk III Cortina had more of a "Detroit look" than its predecessors, with a pronounced "coke-bottle" kick-up over the rear wheels and difficult-to-press ridges extending the front wing tips forward to frame a "more prestigious" grille with – according to model – twin or quad headlamps. And the model line-up was complex: with base, X, XL, GT and GXL trim ranges, 1100cc (export only), 1300cc, 1600cc, 1600cc GT and 2000cc engines (the latter two all-new ohc "Pinto" units with cogged rubber belt camshaft drive), two- and four-door saloon bodywork and four-door estates, the new Cortina was available in "35 basic versions". A pick-up version was only seen in export markets. Typical of Copp was his insistence on "short and long arm" coil and wishbone suspension instead of the simpler MacPherson Strut; 1600 GT and 2000cc models had anti-roll bars.

There were few changes for 1971 – instrument changes on the GT and GXL and sports wheels standardised on the GT – but between February and June 1972 necessary rationalisation was brought to bear on the sprawling model

1971 Cortina 2 litre GXL

1973 Cortina 2000E

Rear view of the Cortina Mk III in 2000E form

1970 Cortina GT had four halogen headlamps and high-back "safety" seats

Side view of the Cortina GT two-door

The 1970 Cortina XL four-door ➤

Fascia layout of the 1970 Cortina XL featured plenty of wood-graining ▼

range. The 2000cc engine was no longer available on base saloons and estates or 2-door L saloons, while the 1300 engine was deleted from XL saloons and estate cars. In June reversing lamps were standardised on all models, while XL, GT and GXL gained hazard flashers.

At the end of the year, Cortina had outsold all other cars on the British market in each month and total sales of 187,159 were a new Ford record.

The rationalisation continued in April 1973 with the deletion of the 1300 base and L estate cars and the 2000cc XL two-door saloon, the 1600GT and the 1600GXL. In the following September there was a major revision of the Mk III range, with a vastly improved instrument panel (it won a Design Council Award in 1974) and front and rear anti-roll bars on all models, the deletion of the 1600cc ohv engine and the replacement of the GXL with a new top-of-the-range model, the 2000E, with Bedford cord upholstery. XL, GT and 2000E all gained rev counters.

A 2000E estate car – Ford's first "executive" estate – appeared in September 1974 while the specification of the 2000 GT was improved the following December.

The range was given its final major facelift in October 1975 when all models gained a new, all-black radiator

The 1970 Cortina
Estate Car

1974 Cortina 2000E
Estate Car

grille, cloth trim, carpet, servo-assisted brakes, heated rear window, hazard flashers and cigar lighter; all estates except the base had rear wash/wipe fitted. The best-selling Cortina L models were now fitted with driver's door mirror, rectangular halogen headlamps, and opening rear quarter windows on two-door models. The XL now had centre console with clock, wood surround instrument panel and intertia reel seat belts.

To crown the season, the millionth Mk III Cortina left the Dagenham production lines on October 21 and the Cortina was Britain's best-seller for the fourth year in succession. There was one last change: in February the Cortina 1300 was fitted with an "economy engine". Production of the Mk III ceased in July 1976.

Produced August 1970 – July 1976

Total production 1,126,559 (includes two-door 143,420, Estate 154,216, Pick-up 4855)

Cortina 1300 1970-76

SPECIFICATION

Engine in-line 1298cc four cylinder ohv
Bore × stroke 80.98×62.99mm
Maximum power 57bhp @ 5500rpm
Transmission four speed manual
Chassis pressed steel monocoque
Wheelbase 101.5in (2580mm)
Track 56.9in (1445mm)
Length 167.7in (4260mm)
Suspension front SLA coil-and-wishbones/rear beam axle with upper and lower trailing arms and coil springs
Brakes four wheel hydraulic, front disc/rear drum
Bodywork two door/four door saloon, estate car
Maximum speed (approx) 85mph (137km/h)

Cortina 1600 OHV 1970-74

Specification as above except:
Engine in-line 1599cc four cylinder ohv
Bore × stroke 80.98×77.62mm
Automatic transmission optional
Maximum power 68bhp @ 5200rpm
Maximum speed (approx) 91mph (146km/h)

Cortina 1600 OHC 1970-76

Specification as above except:
Engine in-line 1593cc four cylinder ohc
Bore × stroke 87.65×66mm
Maximum power 88bhp @ 5700rpm
Maximum speed (approx) 101mph (162km/h)

Cortina 2000 OHC 1970-76

Specification as above except:
Engine in-line 1993cc four cylinder ohc
Bore × stroke 90.8×76.95mm
Maximum power 98bhp @ 5500rpm
Maximum speed (approx) 103mph (166km/h)

1972 Consul L

Rear aspect of the 1972 Consul L

1972 Granada 3000 GXL

Rear view of the GXL Granada shows vinyl roof

Consul/Granada 1972-77

The "MH" range – it stood for "Medium Hummer", a rather odd designation since "Hummer" is German for "lobster" – was developed to replace the disappointing Mk IV Zephyr/Zodiac range with the philosophy "brings large cars down to size". The Consul name was revived for the cheaper models in the range, and was available in three models – base, L and GT – with a choice of V4 2000cc or V6 2500cc engines in base and L, and the 3000cc V6 in the GT, which boasted extra instrumentation including ammeter and oil pressure gauge, a special black grille, halogen driving lamps and sports road wheels.

The Granada was offered in base and GXL models with the 2500 and 3000 engines, but the Granada 2500 was to be dropped in April 1973. The GXL – available only with automatic transmission – had a vinyl roof as standard. Interior equipment on both models was comprehensive though the pushbutton radio – standard on GXL – remained an option on Granada. Estate versions of the Consul 2.5 and Granada appeared in September 1972. For 1974, the base Granada became the XL.

In the early days of Ford's ownership of Ghia, a "customised" Granada called

Consuls on the line at Dagenham

Rare Granada – the two-door Ghia 3 litre Coupé with optional alloy wheels

the "Ghia Mark I" had been shown at the Geneva Salon: with a Lincoln radiator grille and quad headlamps it failed to arouse enthusiasm. However, on 16 January 1974 Ford launched the Granada Ghia, with a distinctive die-cast grille and headlamp surrounds allied to Ghia-designed interior trim; it was not available in Britain until April. It was followed in July by the two-door Granada Ghia Coupé, a fastback five-seater with elegant lines. But though such saloon-derived coupés represented a significant part of the Granada market in Germany, the Coupé's sales in Britain were disappointing. The problem was that though most German Granadas were owner-driven – and thus a two-door car was acceptable – in Britain Granadas were often chauffeur-driven, and thus four-door models were preferred.

In July the 2000cc V4 engine in the Consul was replaced by the ohc 2000cc engine, and the model went on sale in September. The ohc 2 litre was also introduced in Granada models and the Consul Estate in May 1975, but that October the Consul name was laid to rest. The Granada S replaced the Consul GT and the ohc 2 litre engine was additionally offered in the Granada Ghia Saloon and Coupé. A 2 litre ohc Granada "Economy" was launched in February

Distinctive fastback of the Granada Ghia Coupé

Granada L Estate Car

1974 Capri II 1600 XL

J.P.S. Capri II

1976, but that July all Granada production was transferred to Germany since the British output had fallen away dramatically.

Produced December 1971 – July 1976 (Dagenham)/July 1977 (Cologne)

British production 123,368 (Consul 58,969, Consul Estate 6002, Granada 50,747, Granada Estate 7650)

2000cc V4 OHV 1972-74

SPECIFICATION

Engine 1996cc ohv V4
Bore × stroke 93.66×72.42mm
Maximum power 82bhp @ 5000rpm
Transmission four speed/automatic optional
Chassis pressed steel monocoque
Wheelbase 109in (2770mm)
Track 60in (1525mm)
Length 180in (4572mm)
Suspension independent all round: Macpherson strut front/semi-trailing arm rear
Brakes hydraulic, front disc/rear drum
Bodywork two door coupé, four door saloon, estate car
Maximum speed (approx) 92mph (148km/h)

2000cc OHC 1974-77

Specification as above except:
Engine in-line four cylinder 1998cc ohc
Bore × stroke 90.8×76.95mm
Maximum power 99bhp @ 5200rpm
Maximum speed (approx) 100mph (161km/h)

2500cc V6 OHV 1972-77

Specification as above except:
Engine 2495cc V6 ohv
Bore × stroke 93.66×60.35mm
Maximum power 120bhp @ 5300rpm
Maximum speed (approx) 106mph (171km/h)

3000cc V6 OHV 1972-77

Specification as above except:
Engine 2994cc V6 ohv
Bore × stroke 93.66×72.42mm
Maximum power 138bhp @ 5000rpm
Maximum speed (approx) 113mph (182km/h)

Capri Mk II 1974-78

They called the programme to develop the Mk II Capri "Project Diana" after "a secretary in Product Planning who was an inspiration to a lot of people involved in the project!" The original concept had squared-off side windows and pop-up headlamps, but these were rejected by Henry Ford II, who insisted on fixed lamps and an elliptical window line like the Mk I Capri. A major factor which determined the ultimate character of Diana was the shift in Capri sales during the latter days of the Mk I, where German sales declined by a third but sales in Britain were only slightly down. So a car was created that appealed more to the British family market; the result was a blander, heavier car with the added convenience of a hatchback design.

It was launched in January 1974, and the GT version was claimed to be the first hatchback with 50:50 split folding rear seats. They called Capri II "the once in a lifetime car", but the complex range of the Mk I Capri was replaced by three basic models: Capri II L, XL and GT, with 1300 ohv or 1600 ohv engines in L, 1600 ohc in XL and 1600GT, 2000cc ohc in 2000GT and 3000 V6 engines in 3000 GT. The GT could be specified with a "Sports Custom Pack" which included

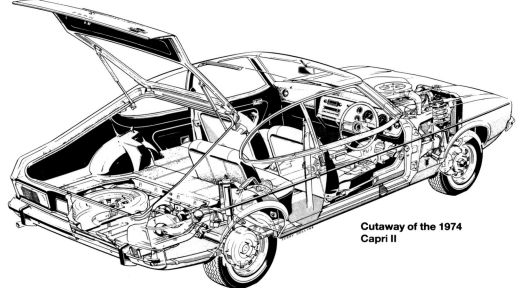

Cutaway of the 1974
Capri II

**The 1974 Capri II
Ghia 3.0**

**The hatchback's
utility was slightly
negated by the
Capri's fastback
styling**

**As sold in the USA,
this 1976 2.3 litre
Capri II has quad
lamps and a ducktail
spoiler**

sports wheels, double coachstripe, map light, overriders and rear wash/wipe.

On April 30th came the luxury Capri II Ghia 2000 and 3000, second European Ford to bear the name of the famous Torinese carrozzeria. Trimmed in Rialto cloth with cut pile carpeting, it had the split-fold rear seats and the rear wash/wipe was standard.

Capri production in 1974, the first year of the new model, was an encouraging 183,700, but this evaporated dramatically in 1975, when German production declined from 36,700 to 20,700.

At the March 1975 Geneva Salon the first "special edition" of the Capri II, the S, was introduced, though it didn't go on sale in Britain until June 10. Available in black with gold striping like the John Player Special grand prix Lotus livery, it became unofficially known as the "JPS" Capri; all the "brightwork" was black, too, as was the interior trim, apart from gold panels on the seats (white "JPS" Capris were also available but rarely seen). Available with 1600GT, 2000GT or 3000GT engines, it initially had special order status and 1750 were sold in this way until the "S" model replaced the GT in the standard range in September. The double body stripe was retained but now a full range of body colours was offered The 1300/1600XL

German-built export version of the Capri IIS with quad headlamps and the 2.8-litre V6 engine which was not yet specified for British-built Capris

were replaced by GL models.

At the same time all models had an upgrade in specification and an "entry-level" base Capri 1300 was added to the range, with fixed-back seats, black bumpers and rubber mats.

In October 1976 British production of the Capri came to an end and from then on all Capris were built in Cologne: production volumes were still falling and Cologne production of Capris for the USA was to end in 1977. That year Cologne made more Capris (91,600) than the previous year but fewer than Halewood and Cologne had built together (101,100) in 1976 . . .

Produced December 1973 – October 1976 (Britain)/January 1978 (Germany)
"JPS" models available June-September 1975
"S" models introduced October 1975
1300 base introduced October 1975

British production 84,400

Capri 1300   1974-78

SPECIFICATION

Engine in-line 1297cc four cylinder ohv
Bore × stroke 80.98×62.99mm
Maximum power 57bhp @ 5500rpm
Transmission four speed
Chassis pressed steel monocoque
Wheelbase 100.75in (2559mm)
Track 53in (1346mm)
Length 171in (4340mm)
Suspension independent MacPherson strut front/semi-elliptic rear
Brakes four wheel hydraulic, discs front/drums rear
Bodywork three-door coupé
Maximum speed (approx) 86mph (138km/h)

Capri 1300GT   1974-78

Specification as above except:
Maximum power 72bhp @ 5500rpm
Maximum speed (approx) 94mph (151km/h)

Capri 1600   1974-78

Specification as above except:
Engine in-line 1593cc four cylinder ohc
Bore × stroke 87.65×66mm

Maximum power 72bhp @ 5500rpm
Transmission four speed/automatic optional
Maximum speed (approx) 93mph (153km/h)

Capri 1600GT   1974-78

Specification as above except:
Maximum power 88bhp @ 5700rpm
Maximum speed (approx) 100mph (161km/h)

Capri 2000GT   1974-78

Specification as above except:
Engine in-line 1998cc four cylinder ohc
Bore × stroke 90.8×76.9mm
Maximum power 98bhp @ 5200rpm
Maximum speed (approx) 108mph (174km/h)

Capri 3000GT   1974-78

Specification as above except:
Engine 2993cc ohv V6
Bore × stroke 93.66×72.42mm
Maximum power 140bhp @ 5300rpm
Maximum speed (approx) 120mph (193km/h)

Mk II version of the Escort L had square headlamps

Escort 1.3L four door

Escort Mk II and its derivatives 1975-80

"Project Brenda" – the 1975 Escort – was named after a secretary in Ford's product development division. Work began in 1972 and the first fruit of the programme, the redesigned floorpan, was incorporated into Mk I production in the latter part of 1973. If Mk I had been a British project that was given a European dimension late in its development, Escort Mk II was very definitely the product of the new Ford of Europe organisation. While its bodywork was substantially a "re-skin" of the earlier model, the Ford of Europe design team headed by Uwe Bahnsen transformed its appearance with more square-cut lines and 23 per cent more glass area, the new look actually giving a couple of inches' extra rear legroom. Estate versions had the new look only back as far as the "A" pillar; from there on they were the same as the Mk I Escort estate.

The complex launch range appeared in January 1975 and encompassed 19 models. Lower series had round sealed-beam headlamps and drum brakes and were available with either 1100cc or 1300cc engines (but only with automatic transmission on the Escort Saloon, which had rubber floor mats). The

slightly better-equipped Escort L had loop pile carpets and a heated rear window. The GL and Ghia saloons had square halogen headlamps and front disc brakes (servo-assisted on 1300GL and 1300 and 1600 Ghia). The Escort Sport – available with 1300GT or 1600 GT engines – also had servo-assisted disc/drum brakes but circular halogen headlamps backed up by halogen driving lamps.

The range was augmented in June by the RS1800, a limited-production successor to the Mk I RS1600 powered by the 1.8 litre dohc BDA engine. Competition RS1800s were created by re-

shelling and re-engining Mk I RS1600 Escorts, while the small batch of road-going RS1800 Escorts was created by re-engineering a fleet of Saarlouis-built Pinto-engined Mexicos in the Pilot Plant at Aveley, and thus their body shells carried German 1.6 litre build codes! Only 109 road-going RS1800 Escorts were registered in Britain between 1975-78.

In response to the straitened times of the mid-1970s, hit by the first oil shock, Ford introduced a new low-priced Escort in July 1975, reviving the name "Popular" for this £1299 two-door (there was also a "Popular Plus").

In October 1975 advance announce-

1979 version of the Escort Ghia

ment was made of Mk II Mexicos and RS2000 Escorts, though these did not go on sale until January 1976. These had been developed at Aveley before the closure of AVO, but were built at Saarlouis; the 2 litre RS2000 was distinguished in road-going form by a polyurethane "beak" grille carrying four headlamps and soft enough to absorb minor impacts (though many competition cars had the flat front and quarter bumpers of the Mexico). Four spoke alloy "RS" wheels were initially standard but became an option later; the Mexico failed to live up to sales expectations so in September 1978 it (and the RS1800) was withdrawn and the cheaper interior of the Mk II Mexico was fitted in the RS2000 body to create a steel-wheeled RS2000. At the same time an RS2000 Custom, with Recaro seats, alloy wheels and higher equipment specification, was introduced.

Another sporty Escort, the four-door Escort Sport, had been discontinued in May 1976. In July-August 1978, a "Special Edition" Escort 1.6L was offered; it used the mechanicals of the Escort Sport. A revised Escort range appeared in September 1978; from this point on, various "limited editions" made their appearance, the first of these the 1300cc Escort Capital, an edition of 1000 cars sponsored by London Ford dealers (600

Cockpit of the 1979 Escort Sport

1979 Escort 1600 Sport ▼

Unique front-end styling of the Escort RS2000

YHJ 754T

The 1975 Escort 1.3 Estate

were painted Capital Red and 400 were Light Orchid) which was offered in May 1979. That October the Escort L and GL were offered with the 1600 Sport power unit; 1600 examples of a "special" version of the L and GL painted Dark Blue were built. November 1979 saw the Escort Linnet, derived from the 1100cc and 1300cc four-door Popular Plus; 5000 were made.

In January/February 1980 came the Escort Harrier, an edition of 1500 cars derived from the 1600 Sport and fitted with Recaro seats, rear spoiler and alloy RS wheels to commemorate such motorsport achievements as the Escort's eighth successive victory in the RAC Rally. Finished as standard in white with a distinctive blue triple side-stripe (irreverently known as "High-speed Gas" from its similarity to the British Gas logo), it was available at extra cost in Strato Silver.

In May 1980 came the Escort Huntsman Estate, a limited (350 units) edition sold by South-Eastern dealers, while the Escort Goldcrest (2000 units) introduced the following month was derived from the Escort L, finished in Sable Brown and Gold, and powered by either the 1300cc or 1600cc engines. In August 1980, right at the end of the Mk II Escort's production run, came the Escort Linnet Plus, of which just 1500

**Escort Mexico Mk II
1976-78**

**Escort RS1800 1975-
1980**

examples were built in two- and four-door form, with either the 1100cc or 1300cc power units.

Produced December 2, 1974 – midsummer 1980
Halewood production 960,007
Saarlouis production 848,388
UK registrations of Mk II RS Escorts: RS 2000 10,039, RS1800 109, Mexico 2290 (approx)

Escort 1100 1974-80

SPECIFICATION

Engine in-line ohv 1098cc four cylinder
Bore × stroke 81×53.3mm
Maximum power 53bhp @ 5500rpm
Transmission four speed
Chassis pressed steel monocoque
Wheelbase 94.5in (2400mm)
Track 50in (1270mm)
Length 157in (3988mm)
Suspension independent MacPherson strut front/semi-elliptic rear
Brakes four wheel hydraulic (front discs on 1300cc and over)
Bodywork two door/four door saloon, estate car
Maximum speed (approx) 84mph (135km/h)

Escort 1300 1974-80

Specification as above except:
Engine in-line ohv 1298cc four-cylinder
Bore × stroke 81×63mm
Maximum power 63bhp @ 5300rpm
Maximum speed (approx) 88mph (142km/h)

Escort 1300GT 1974-80

Specification as above except:
Maximum power 72bhp @ 6000rpm
Maximum speed (approx) 93mph (150km/h)

Escort 1600 Sport 1974-80

Specification as above except:
Engine in-line 1599cc ohv four-cylinder
Bore × stroke 80.98×62.99mm
Maximum power 84bhp @ 6000rpm
Maximum speed (approx) 103mph (166km/h)

Escort RS1800 1975-1980

Specification as above except:
Engine in-line 1834cc four-cylinder 16 valve BDA dohc
Bore × stroke 86.75×77.62mm
Maximum power 115bhp @ 6000rpm
Maximum speed (approx) 111mph (179km/h)

Escort RS Mexico Mk II 1976-78

Specification as above except:
Engine in-line ohv 1593cc four-cylinder
Bore × stroke 87.67×66mm
Maximum power 95bhp @ 5750rpm
Maximum speed (approx) 106mph (170km/h)

Escort RS2000 Mk II 1978-79

Specification as above except:
Engine in-line ohc 1993cc four-cylinder
Bore × stroke 90.82×76.95mm
Power output 110bhp @ 5500rpm
Maximum speed (approx) 109mph (175km/h)

1977 Cortina 2.3 with optional alloy wheels

Front view of the 1976 Cortina 1.6 GL

Rear aspect of the Mk IV Cortina 1.6 GL

Cortina Mk IV 1976-82

Launched in September 1976, the Mk IV Cortina range was another of Uwe Bahnsen's skilful re-skinnings of an existing model, in this case combining the Mk III Cortina and the mechanically similar but externally different Taunus from Germany (and so Mk IVs built on the Continent were badged "Taunus", a name that went back to the late 1930s). Lower and squarer than its predecessor, the Mk IV Cortina had a greater glass area, an integral front spoiler and revised front suspension.

Power units were 1300cc, 1600cc and 2000cc. An economy version of the 1.6 litre engine was standard on the base model, optional on the Cortina L. A new Cortina S replaced the GT model in the range and the Cortina Ghia made its debut as the top of the range model. Both models were powered by the 2000cc Pinto engine and had centre console, pushbutton radio, head restraints, gas dampers, clock, intermittent wipe and sports road wheels. Though the Cortina was edged out of top place in the UK market by the Escort in 1976, it was to be Britain's best seller from 1977 to 1981.

In September 1977 the 2.3 litre V6 was added to the list of available engines

1980 Cortina two-door base model

Interior of the 1980 Cortina Ghia

1980 Cortina L four ▲ door

▲ The 1980 Cortina GL

Interior of the 1980 Cortina L

**1980 Cortina L
Estate**

**1980 Cortina Ghia
Estate**

for GL, Ghia and S variants of the Cortina; it came together with power steering, firmer suspension and higher gearing. Power steering was optional on 2000cc Cortinas and a 1600cc Ghia was added to the range.

Only detail modifications occurred until the launch of the 1980 Cortina range – unofficially known as "MkV" – in August 1979. With increased glass area, laminated windscreen, a new grille with aerofoil slats, new seats and better ventilation, the new range featured a number of engine improvements including variable venturi carburettors

on the 1300 and 1600 models, viscous-coupling radiator fans to reduce power loss, transistorised ignition on 2.3 models and major service intervals increased to 12,000 miles. The Cortina S vanished as a separate model, to be replaced by an S "handling pack" available on L, GL and Ghia models.

Cortina did not altogether escape the "limited edition" syndrome and in May 1980 South-Eastern dealers launched the Cortina Huntsman estate, of which just 150 were built. More detail improvements were made in July 1980 and in January 1981 an "added value"

programme typically saw extras worth £230 added to the Ghia at no extra cost.

In June the Cortina Carousel special edition appeared in 1300cc and 1600cc guise with sports wheels and Ghia-type seats; 6000 of this first Carousel were built. A further 2200 Carousels to 1982 specification would be built from August 1982; changes across the range included adjustable headrests on all models except the base, revised fascias on the L and a higher specification on the Ghia. All models could be ordered with twin "Econolites" which reacted to inlet manifold depression and lit up to

**Completion of the 4
millionth Cortina**

**Last of the Cortina
line, the 1982
Crusader**

1980 Cortina GLS

warn when the engine was operating
uneconomically (the author recalls one
high-speed dash across Belgium to
catch a ferry when both Econolites were
alight most of the time!).

To round off Cortina production, in
May 1982 the Cortina Crusader
appeared, based on 1300, 1600 and
2000cc saloons and estates. With such
extras as sports wheels, remote control
door mirrors and centre console, the
Crusader had a production run of
30,000 units.

The last Cortina was driven off the
Dagenham production line by Ford of
Britain's Sam Toy on July 22, 1982 and is
now preserved in Ford's small
collection of historic vehicles; however,
the "Cortina line" lived on for some
time in the shape of the South African
P100 pickup, which went on sale in
Britain in June 1982 and used the front-
end body pressings of the Cortina on a
chassis frame.

Produced September 1976 – August 1979
(MkIV)/August 1979 – September 1982
(MkV)

Total production 1,131,850

1980 Cortina Ghia

Cortina 1300   1976-82

SPECIFICATION

Engine in-line 1298cc four cylinder
ohv
Bore × stroke 80.98×62.99mm
Maximum power 60bhp @
5000rpm
Transmission four speed/automatic
optional
Chassis pressed steel monocoque
Wheelbase 101.5in (2578mm)
Track 56.9in (1445mm)
Length 170.35in (4327mm)
Suspension independent
MacPherson strut front/semi-elliptic
rear
Brakes hydraulic, front disc/rear
drum
Bodywork two door, four door
saloon, estate car
Maximum speed (approx) 82mph
(137km/h)

Cortina 1600 ohv   1976-82

Specification as above except:
Engine 1599cc ohv
Bore × stroke 80.98×77.62mm
Maximum power 71bhp @
4500rpm
Maximum speed (approx) 88mph
(146km/h)

Cortina 1600 ohc   1976-82

Specification as above except:
Engine in-line 1593cc four cylinder
ohc
Bore × stroke 87.65×66mm
Maximum power 86bhp @
5000rpm
Maximum speed (approx) 94mph
(162km/h)

Cortina 2000   1976-82

Specification as above except:
Engine in-line 1993cc four cylinder
ohc
Bore × stroke 90.8×76.95mm
Maximum power 102bhp @
5400rpm
Maximum speed (approx) 103mph
(166km/h)

Cortina 2.3   1977-82

Specification as above except:
Engine 2296cc V6 ohv
Bore × stroke 90×60.1mm
Maximum power 116bhp @
5500rpm
Maximum speed (approx) 106mph
(171km/h)

The 1977 Fiesta L

First Dagenham-built Fiesta ➤

Henry Ford II test-drives a prototype Fiesta, 1976

Fiesta MkI   1976-84

Ford's bold decision to build the Fiesta confounded some of the most deeply entrenched wisdoms of the motor industry – "mini car, mini profits" or "you can't build a new model in a new factory in a new country" – for, in addition to the established Ford plants in Britain and Germany, the Fiesta was to be built in a brand-new factory in Spain, where the previous Ford plant had closed as a direct result of the Civil War four decades earlier.

The basic shape of what was to become the Fiesta was created in the studio of Ford's new Italian acquisition, Ghia, by designer Tom Tjaarda (whose father had created the immortal Lincoln Zephyr for Ford US in the 1930s). But there was input from all round the Ford world into the remarkable little Fiesta, which broke much new ground for Ford: it was the company's first front-wheel drive car, the first with a transverse engine, and it had the smallest engine Ford had built since the 8hp Anglia had gone out of production in the 1950s. Moreover, though the project – codenamed "Bobcat" – coincided with the first great oil shock, Ford management decided to plough ahead with it at undiminished speed. The power unit,

1977 Fiesta S

**Interior of the
original Fiesta S**

**Rear view of the
1977 Fiesta Ghia**

though it bore a family resemblance to the "Kent" series, had a new cylinder block that was more than an inch shorter, with 74mm bores, and with only three main bearings.

The launch range was 957cc (in high or low compression ratio form) or 1117cc. Though the Fiesta was available on the Continent in the third quarter of 1976, it was not launched in Britain until February 1977, in 957cc base, 957 or 1117cc L, 1117cc S, 957 or 1117cc Ghia forms. A 1298cc engine was added to the range in September 1977; the Fiesta 1300 was only available in S or Ghia models, the S having unique sidestripes incorporating a 1300 S motif.

The first special edition Fiesta appeared in August 1978 to celebrate the 75th anniversary of Ford Motor Company (which had actually happened on June 16); 2000 were built. In December came the Fiesta Kingfisher (2500 built) and in March 1979, the Fiesta Million marked the building of the millionth example of this phenomenally successful minicar. Based on the L, the Fiesta Million ran to 3100 units. The Fiesta Sandpiper of December 1979 was again L-based, and 2500 were built. The enterprising Gates Group created the Fiesta Jubilee in January 1980 to mark their 60 years as Ford dealers; there were just 60 Jubilees, 30 Apollo Green, 30 Midnight Blue.

In February the Fiesta GL was added to the range, with 1100 and 1300cc engines. More special editions appeared towards the end of the year: the Firefly (2000 built) came out in July, the 4000-off Festival, derived from the 957 and 1100cc base Fiesta, appeared in September, and 3000 Fiesta Supersports based on the 1300S were built in October; the model went into the mainstream catalogue from February to August 1981.

The Popular and Popular Plus were in the catalogues by December 1980, available with 957cc low or high compression engines; the 1100 was an option in the Popular Plus, which had cloth instead of plastic trim, carpet instead of rubber matting. The Fiesta Sandpiper II of March 1981, finished in Roman Bronze/Solar Gold, ran to 4000 units and differed little from its 1979 predecessor.

The L-derived Fiesta Bravo of June

The base model 1977 Fiesta

New for 1978 – the Fiesta 1300S

1981 first appeared in 957cc form but after 64 had been built, the 1100 and 1300cc engines were used and production reached 3000 units. Also in June, the Fiesta 1300L – a 2000-car run – was launched, then, in September the Fiesta appeared in mildly facelifted form.

The 1600cc Fiesta XR2 was launched in December. April 1982 saw Fiesta Economy with revised gearbox and final drive ratios, a thermostatic fan as standard on 957cc Fiestas and the 4000-off Fiesta Bravo II. The Fiesta Carnival, based on the Fiesta Popular and 957 and 1100 Economy models, was built in an edition of 3000 in December. The Fiesta Quartz ("Timed to Perfection") appeared in January and 7000 were built. In April the Fiesta Finesse – derived from the L – proved the biggest special run of all, for 12,000 were manufactured. September saw the launch of the 1984 Fiesta with more rounded lines front and rear.

Produced 1976-83 (Britain)

Total British production 307,600

Fiesta 1976-84

SPECIFICATION

Engine transverse 957cc in-line four cylinder ohv
Bore × stroke 74×55.7mm
Maximum power 40bhp @ 5500rpm (LC)/45bhp @ 6000rpm (HC)
Transmission four speed transaxle
Chassis pressed steel monocoque
Wheelbase 90in (2286mm)
Track 52.5in (1345mm)
Length 140.4in (3566mm)
Suspension MacPherson strut front/dead beam axle with trailing arms and coil springs rear
Brakes hydraulic, front disc/rear drum
Bodywork three door hatchback
Maximum speed (approx) 80mph (129km/h)/85mph (137km/h)

Fiesta 1100 1976-84

Specification as above except:
As above except:
Capacity 1117cc
Bore × stroke 74mm×65mm
Maximum power 53bhp @ 6000rpm
Maximum speed (approx) 90mph (145km/h)

Fiesta 1300 1977-84

SPECIFICATION

As above except:
Capacity 1298cc
Bore × stroke 81mm×63mm
Maximum power 66bhp @ 6000rpm
Maximum speed (approx) 98mph (158km/h)

Fiesta XR2 1981-84

Specification as above except:
Capacity 1598cc
Bore × stroke 81×77.6mm
Maximum power 84bhp @ 5500rpm
Maximum speed (approx) 106mph

The 1977 Ford range fully kitted out with Series X conversions

Series X RS2000 "feels just like my rally car" commented works driver Björn Waldegaard

A standard 1977 Capri with Series X body kit

"Series X"

In August 1977 Ford announced a scheme called "Series X"; its aim was "to ensure that Ford owners are at the fore-front of the customising scheme". By selecting kits of parts from the lengthy RS catalogue, owners could improve the braking, handling and appearance of their Fiestas, Escorts, Capris and even Cortinas.

The kits – composed of "parts that are known to work well together" – included carburettors and camshafts to improve performance and springs and dampers for tauter handling. But the parts which made the most visible difference were extended wheelarches to permit the fitting of extra-wide alloy wheels and airdams and spoilers.

What made Series X kits "semi-production" was the fact that they could only be fitted by dealers; thus there were no concerns about safety or legality. Series X kits could be ordered at the same time as the car – so that it was delivered equipped to the customer's specifications. Available for Capri 3000S were an engine kit to uprate power output from 138 to 170bhp; limited-slip differential; ventilated disc brakes; alloy 7½ × 13in wheels for 225/60 tyres; stiffer suspension with gas-filled struts; air

1977 Series X Fiesta 1100S

dam and spoiler; and "Spa" type glass fibre wheelarches.

For those to whom image was more important than performance, "much of the above equipment and in particular the cosmetic items can also be fitted to the smaller-engined Capris," said Ford.

A similar philosophy was applied to the Series X kit intended for the Escort RS2000, which included Group One engine kit; Rocket close-ratio gearbox; limited-slip diffential; ventilated discs; 7½ × 13in alloy wheels; "Tour of Britain specification" suspension; high-ratio steering rack; front airdam and rear spoiler; and "Zakspeed" style wheelarches. Ford ingenuously commented: "Of course some of these options, particularly the cosmetic ones, may be fitted to other Escort Models, including the

Populars."

Series X modifications which had no mainstream sporting equivalents were those offered for the Fiesta and Cortina. The Series X Fiesta extras included 7.00 × 13in RS wheels instead of the standard 12in units (this permitted the fitting of larger diameter discs), matt black polyurethane wheelarches and air dam, and an engine kit for the Fiesta 1100 which was said to raise power output by over 20 per cent. For Cortina, Ford candidly admitted: "Though there is less call for go-faster accessories to fit Ford's best-seller than say the sportier Escort or Capri, an air dam, rear spoiler, 6in alloy wheels and special gas-filled dampers are available for all versions of this car." The number of Series X conversions carried out is unknown.

1978 Granada L

**The 1978 Granada, in
S and Ghia models**

Granada GL interior

Granada Mk II   1977-85

Yet again, the classically square-cut Mk II Granada represented a skilful re-skin by the designers under Uwe Bahnsen and completed the "family look" of the Ford car range. Granadas were now all built in Germany and both saloons and estate cars were introduced at the same time, in August 1977. "Emphasis on engineering" was the thrust of the launch, and extensive changes were made to the engine line-up. New in the Granada were the 2.3 and 2.8 litre V6 units, with electronic ignition and the option of fuel injection on the larger unit, plus a new 2.1 litre diesel.

The model range was complex, consisting of Diesel, L, GL, S and Ghia saloons, plus L and GL estates; the S, with standard fuel injection, Bilstein gas shock absorbers and sports suspension, was the shortest-lived variant, for it survived only until September 1978, when it was replaced by "S-packs" which were optional on GL and Ghia models with carburettors but standard on fuel injected cars. The Ghia estate was introduced without publicity during 1978.

In June 1979 came the limited-edition Granada Sapphire, finished in Midnight Blue/Strato Silver. It was based on the

Ghia with S-pack suspension and Michelin TRX wheels and tyres, and 1725 were built (plus 28 for Ford Motor Company which omitted the S-pack and the TRX wheels and tyres).

In June 1980 came perhaps the best-known special-edition Granada, the Chasseur, based either on the normally aspirated 2.8 litre Granada Estate with

The 1978 Granada GL with optional vinyl roof

**The 1979 Granada
Ghia Estate**

automatic transmission (standard) or optionally on the 2.8i Estate with manual gearbox. It was finished in two-tone Roman Bronze/Tuscan Beige with a gold pinstripe, and had gold-finished alloy wheels with TRX tyres and interior trim in bitter chocolate leather with Chatham check fabric inserts. In the load compartment were four specially-made holdalls in – sadly – simulated leather. Just 500 Chasseurs were built.

In November came the 800-off Granada Talisman, based on the 2.0 ohc and 2.3 V6 Granada L. The Granada was facelifted in September 1981; before that, in July, the Granada Consort had been offered, in an edition of 1500.

Produced (Cologne only) December 1976-1985

Total production 639,440

2000cc 1977-85

SPECIFICATION

Engine in-line four cylinder 1998cc ohc
Bore × stroke 90.8×76.95mm
Maximum power 99bhp @ 5200rpm
Transmission four speed/automatic optional
Chassis pressed steel monocoque
Wheelbase 109in (2770mm)
Track 60in (1525mm)
Length 182in (4623mm)
Suspension independent all round: Machpherson strut front/semi-trailing arm rear
Brakes hydraulic, front disc/rear drum
Bodywork four door saloon, estate car
Maximum speed (approx) 102mph (164km/h)

2100cc Diesel 1977-85

Specification as above except:
Engine in-line four cylinder 2112cc Diesel ohv
Bore × stroke 90×83mm
Maximum power 63bhp @ 4500rpm
Maximum speed (approx) 85mph (137km/h)

2300cc V6 1977-85

Specification as above except:
Engine 2293cc ohv V6
Bore × stroke 90.03×60.14mm
Maximum power 108bhp @ 5000rpm
Maximum speed (approx) 105mph (169km/h)

2800cc V6 1977-85

Specification as above except:
Engine 2792cc ohv V6
Bore × stroke 93×68.5mm
Maximum power 135bhp @ 5200rpm
Maximum speed (approx) 113mph (182km/h)

2800cc V6 FI 1977-85

Specification as above except:
Maximum power 160bhp @ 5700rpm
Maximum speed (approx) 120mph (193km/h)

1978 Capri GL had sports wheels

1978 Capri L

Capri Mk III   1978-1987

In keeping with the Capri tradition, the MkIII was codenamed "Carla"; a new louvred aerofoil grille incorporating quad headlamps, an integral chin spoiler and a redesigned bonnet made a significant improvement to the car's aerodynamics as well as giving the car a more sporting appearance. This "New Look Capri" had wide rubbing strakes on all models except the base 1.3 litre Saloon and the S (which had a wide "strobe" decal incorporating an "S" motif).

All models except the Saloon had Bilstein gas shock absorbers; the L came with either the 1300 ohv or 1600 ohc engines, GL was available with 1600 or 2000cc ohc power units, S came with 1600 or 2000cc ohc fours or the 3000cc V6 (with which power steering was standard) and the Ghia had either the 2000cc ohc or 3000cc V6 engine. It had a sunshine roof and leather-covered steering wheel as standard.

In February 1980 came the 1600cc Capri GT4, of which 1500 units were

**Side stripe marked
1978 Capri S**

built, while in June that year the 1600S was given the standard 1.6 litre engine instead of the 1600GT unit, which was discontinued.

Just outside the scope of this book comes the Capri 2.8i, launched in July 1981, but this new high-performance model developed by Ford's Special Vehicle Engineering division (based at Dunton) was to be the lifeline of the Capri range.

The very last Capri model of all, the special edition 280 of 1987 (sometimes known as the Capri Brooklands because it was only available in Brooklands Green in tribute to the first purpose-built motor race circuit) was the ultimate expression of this low-slung 130mph bolide.

Other latterday Capri "specials" were the February 1981 Capri LS, the August 1981 Capri Calypso based on the 1600LS (1500 built) and its contemporary the 1300/1600cc Capri Cameo (also 1500 built), the March 1982 L-based Capri Cabaret 1600 and 2000 (4000 were built in all), the 1600LS-based May 1982 Calypso II (1500 built), the December 1982 Cabaret II (2000 were made, with the 2.0 litre engine optional), the June 1984 Capri Laser, based on Capri 1.6LS 1600 and 2000, with five-speed gearbox and alloy wheels (total production 6500) and the September 1984 Injection

Special, with limited-slip diff, leather trim and alloy wheels. The Capri Tickford of September 1983 was a joint Ford-Aston Martin venture assembled at Milton Keynes.

Produced (Cologne only) March 1978 – December 1986

Total Capri production (Mks I, II, III) 1,886,647

Capri 1300   1978-86

SPECIFICATION

Engine in-line four cylinder ohv
Bore × stroke 80.98×62.99mm
Maximum power 57bhp @ 5500rpm
Transmission four speed
Chassis pressed steel monocoque
Wheelbase 100.75in (2559mm)
Track 53in (1345mm)
Length 168in (4267mm)
Suspension independent MacPherson strut front/semi-elliptic rear
Brakes hydraulic, disc front/drum rear
Bodywork two door coupé
Maximum speed (approx) 87mph (140km/h)

Capri 1600 1978-86

Specification as above except:
Engine in-line 1593cc four cylinder ohc
Bore × stroke 87.65×66mm
Maximum power 72bhp @ 5500rpm
Transmission four speed/automatic optional
Maximum speed (approx) 99mph (159km/h)

Capri 1600 GT 1978-80

Specification as above except:
Maximum power 88bhp @ 5700rpm
Maximum speed (approx) 104mph (167km/h)

Capri 2000

Specification as above except:
Engine in-line 1993cc four cylinder ohc
Bore × stroke 90.82×76.95mm
Maximum power 98bhp @ 5200rpm
Maximum speed (approx) 110mph (177km/h)

Capri 3000 S

Specification as above except:
Engine 2993cc V6 ohv
Bore × stroke 93.67×72.42mm
Maximum power 138bhp @ 5000rpm
Maximum speed (approx) 122mph (196km/h)

1981 Capri 2.8 Injection